Little Old Dog Sanctuary
Happily Ever After

by

Hope Morgan

Original Copyright © 2014 Misfit Mountain Media

Under ISBN: 978-0-9906647-0-3

Second Edition

Revised Copyright © 2017 Misfit Mountain Media

ISBN: 978-0-9906647-1-0

www.littleolddogsanctuary.org

To Orville, the tiny dog that started it all.

Table of Contents

Once Upon A Time...

Welcome! My name is Hope and I'd like to invite you to take a little peek inside our lives at Little Old Dog Sanctuary.

Our Sanctuary is our home in the little mountain town of Conifer, Colorado. It is a family affair, which consists of me, my super-supportive and somewhat crazy husband, Erik, and my lovely and eccentric son, Oliver. We have four beautiful acres of land, though most of our dogs prefer to be indoors. We have cool summers and long snowy winters. Our home has giant windows to let in the abundant sunlight, and we have a wood burning stove that creates an extremely popular napping area from September through May. In short, we live in a beautiful, magical microcosm of unconditional love, support, and more love all at 9,000 feet above sea level.

Little Old Dog Sanctuary is a sanctuary for small senior and "special needs" dogs that we acquire from county shelters. Our dogs come from all over Colorado and occasionally out of state. We are not a rescue, but rather a Sanctuary, the difference being that we don't adopt our dogs out; once they come in the door, they stay here with us for the remainder of their lives. Technically, we are a hospice. But it's much more pleasant to describe it as "a super-duper-awesome end-of-life utopia wonderland." When we established our free-range, nap encouraging, do-what-you-want, non-judgmental special little world up here, we seem to have inadvertently created an environment where old dogs become young again. Or so it seems. We think it is because of all the unconditional love. Or the lack of oxygen. Or both.

Our lives are busy, exciting, chaotic, overwhelming, crazy and full of joy and purpose. We hope this book gives you a little laugh and helps you look at old dogs in a whole new light. And I also hope it imparts on you the one true key to happiness... an old, messed-up Chihuahua. It's really that simple. And the good news is that there are plenty of them out there, so go grab yourself one or two. And even though we've just given away this life secret in the introduction to our book, you should still go ahead and read the rest of it anyway.

Inna' Beginning

So I never intentionally set out to rescue dogs. I fell into the whole thing quite by accident, really. Don't get me wrong, I've always loved animals. Even from a really young age. I was always bringing home strays, trying to sneak the family dog into my bed at night, begging to keep the cat that was hanging around the neighborhood. But dog rescue hadn't really entered my mind.

My first dachshund was a little dog named Folgers. I bought Folgers from a breeder. I know, I know, but I really didn't know any better at the time. Keep in mind this was long ago. I had looked through the newspaper and had found an ad that looked interesting. Yes, that's right. The newspaper. The Rocky Mountain News. This is how you got a dog back then. Well, either that, or a pet shop. There were a few shelters around, but not many rescues. According to the newspaper ad, there was a woman in Limon selling purebred dachshunds. I had never had one before, but I had been around them some and they seemed brave, intelligent and fun.

So I drove to Limon and bought my first dachshund. Folgers was a fairly normal dog. He was very active, could sit up and do "High Fives," and loved, I mean loved, to swim. So, not only was Folgers "normal," but he would actually be considered talented and extra-ordinary. Had I just stopped with Folgers and not gotten any more dogs, I don't know that I would be doing what I do today.

Peabody was my second dog. I had recently moved to Texas and I foolishly thought that Folgers, with all of his energy and brilliance, needed a friend to share his energy and brilliance with. This is never a good idea. Never, never, never. Ever. It never works out…so don't do it. I know you will, but you've been warned.

I found Peabody on a website similar to Craigslist. This was way back in 1999 before Craigslist existed, but at least it seemed like it was one step above the newspaper. Pea was just a puppy. His current owners were a young couple, recently married, who had never had a dog before. They purchased Peabody in a grocery store parking lot from a backyard breeder. When I met them, it was night four of being up all night with a puppy, and they were more than willing to forego their commitment to dog ownership. Which actually turned out to be a fortuitous decision on their part. By the time Pea died at the young age of seven, he suffered from hypothyroidism, epilepsy, a blown out disk resulting in paralysis, liver damage, diabetes, kidney damage, pancreatitis, a near fatal spider bite and a rare adrenal gland disease. So, if they weren't able to handle him whining for a few nights I'm not sure they would have been equipped to deal with what was to come. But lucky for them, the Universe stepped in.

I guess they didn't know that if you try to put an eight-week old puppy in a crate, alone, in another room, it is probably going to cry. And, if you are going to attempt this method of training, you are going to be in for at least a few nights, or weeks, of crying. I am pretty sure that they expected after one night for their dog to be totally adjusted to its new environment and be potty trained and go out and catch its own meals and maybe even get a part time job to help pay the bills. They weren't willing to put in the work to get from point A to point B to point C to point D. They wanted to go from point A to "Lassie."

But, at this time in my life, I couldn't blame them. I had been naïve and foolish, too. When I first got Folgers at eight weeks, I put him in the bathroom with the door shut to try to get him used to sleeping alone. My ex-husband didn't want dogs sleeping in the bed. After trying to ignore his barking for two hours straight, I went into the bathroom and discovered he had shredded an entire roll of toilet paper and torn up the newspaper he was supposed to be going potty on. So, I decided to put him in a box inside of the bathroom. It was a huge box that came from our new dishwasher. It was about four feet tall. I put him in the box and went back to bed. I listened to Folgers bark for three agonizing hours…you have to understand I'm more of a Dr. Sears kind of girl, not a Dr. Spock kind of girl. Finally I couldn't take it anymore. I went into the bathroom and was shocked at what I found. Folgers was out of the box and in the toilet, arms on each side of the seat, hanging on for his life. He was soaking wet, freezing, shaking and so very, very upset. I felt horrible. I gave him a warm bath and he slept in the bed from then on, despite the protest from my ex-husband. And just as a side note…I never once put my baby in a crib by himself, either. The concept of letting something "cry it out" doesn't exist in my life. As far as I'm concerned, there will be plenty of things to cry over in this lifetime. I don't see why it is necessary to add any more reasons if they can be avoided.

Anyway, back to Peabody. This poor couple was sleep deprived and just wanting little Peabody out of their life so they could go to bed. I remember when I first set eyes on Pea. He cocked his head to the side and just stared at me. The woman told me he had never once barked in the whole time they have had him. The woman just frowned and shook her head from side to side like some sort of sleep-deprived metronome. She said that he would just cry and cry and cry. And then, when they thought that he was finally done, he would take a deep breath and cry some more. As soon as she finished her sentence I looked over at Peabody and he looked me straight in the eyes and barked at me. I picked him up and took him home.

Folgers hated Peabody. Much like your firstborn tries to persuade you to take your second born back to wherever he came from, Folgers made an effort to let us know that anything Pea could do, he could do better. There was no need for a second dog. In fact, a second dog will only take up more of our time and money. And boy, was he right about that. I think Pea's picture was in the Guinness Book of World Records for the dog having the most simultaneous life-threatening maladies and still being alive. For five years in a row. And there was no way that Folgers would allow Peabody to sleep in his bed with his owners. Besides, Folgers had already blazed the trail for the privilege of sleeping in the bed by nearly dying in a toilet. What did Pea ever do to earn rights to the Sealy Posturepedic? Crying at the old owners and barking for the new one? So what?

All this led me to getting a friend for Peabody. I got Orville. And this is how my life snowballed into dog rescue. I found Orville by doing an internet search for dachshund puppies in Texas. I found this glorious web site that was selling purebred dachshund puppies at astronomical prices. They were offering these exotic colors I had never seen before. Obviously there was a reason I had never seen them before…they really didn't exist naturally in nature as nature had intended. They were mutations. And trying to get these strange colors and patterns isn't good for the dog. But back then I was naïve and ignorant. Both my dachshunds were just plain old red. I wanted something really different, and this seemed like the perfect place to find just that. I called the woman who invited me to her house to pick out a dog. She lived in a very remote part of Texas. Really out in the middle of nowhere. It was about a three hour drive from where I lived. I will never forget that day for as long as I live. I had no idea that a simple trip to pick out a puppy would change the course of my life forever. It was the defining moment that made me who and what I am today.

I remember being very excited on the drive. The web site had pictures of green grass and rolling hills with a white picket fence. I had visions of happy, healthy dachshunds running free, barking, playing and frolicking in the sunshine. As I started to get closer to

6

the "puppy haven" I couldn't help but think that something wasn't quite right. Had I taken a wrong turn somewhere? But I was trying to be optimistic thinking that just around the next bend would be a beautiful dachshund farm perched pristinely upon a hill. But all I was seeing now was dirt. Just flat, cracked, baking dirt as far as the eye could see. Not a tree or bush in sight.

When I had finally reached my destination (according to the directions the woman had given me) I sat in the car in total state of shock. Or disbelief. Or denial. Or all of the above. In front of me sat a very old, dilapidated, dirty trailer. It was literally just sitting in the middle of nowhere, propped up on cinder blocks. Don't get me wrong, I have nothing against trailers. In fact, I sort of love them. My grandparents had lived in a trailer when I was growing up. It was the most beautiful, exotic, wonderful home I had ever seen. I loved it. They took great pride in how it looked, and it even had a little Koi pond out front. Sure, it was small, but in my eyes, and in theirs, it was a tiny paradise. But this trailer was not a tiny paradise. It was run-down and filthy. I try not to judge a book by its cover no matter how bad the cover looks, so I gathered my courage, got out of the car and made my way up the rickety steps.

Now maybe it is just me, but I'm always fascinated by people who have no shame. It isn't that I'm a snob or anything, but if I lived in a place like this woman lived I would never let anyone come over. I just wouldn't be able to do it. I wouldn't be able to handle that kind of embarrassment. But, some people have no shame...and Jane Doe was obviously one of those people.

I knocked on the screen door which was only attached by the top hinge, not the bottom. So when you knocked, the screen door sort of slammed into the wooden door behind it. A wooden door that had a huge hole at the bottom, like someone had kicked it in. Immediately after knocking, I heard it. I heard the deafening cacophony of a thousand dachshunds barking and howling. It was the noise that was to become the theme song to my life for the next fifteen years. A noise that has become so familiar to me now that I can sometimes totally block it out. But, honestly, that first

7

time I heard it, it scared me to death. Then I saw her. And this scared me even more. The woman who would haunt my nightmares and become my arch nemesis for the rest of my life. She was a small woman in height. What she lacked in height, she made up for in girth. What I was immediately struck by besides her small stature (she couldn't have been over five feet tall) was the fact that she had a black eye and was missing most of her teeth. She wore a stained, dirty "house dress" and her gray hair stuck out in every direction like she had just crawled out of bed…a bed that was located somewhere in the middle of the sixth level of Hell.

She introduced herself and invited me in. She wasn't particularly nice, warm or welcoming. Nor was she mean or rude…she was just sort of, well, milquetoast. She had a very monotone voice, she shuffled when she walked…she was actually quite zombie-ish really. Upon reflection, knowing she is just a soulless shell possessed by the devil, the entire situation makes perfect sense. But on this day, I hadn't realized this yet. She made brief mention that she had a husband and that he wasn't here right now, but would be home soon. Looking back, I presume he was busy pouring salt into the wounds of lepers and giving cancer to orphans.

Now if Jane Doe could be accurately defined as dirty and unkempt, her house was downright unsanitary. Jane was a hoarder. Not only of dachshunds, but of newspapers, trash and piles of boxes. There was a very small path that led to her kitchen. Upon entering her kitchen there were cages stacked from the floor to the ceiling. In each cage were litters of puppies. There had to have been at least fifty puppies. The kitchen reeked of burning food and stale cigarettes. The first dog I saw was this little red and white dappled dachshund. She had the largest eyes I had ever seen and was just standing there wagging her tail. I guess I noticed her first because her cage just happened to be at my eye level when I walked into the kitchen. She was one of Jane's breeder dogs. She was nursing a litter of five pups. But then I noticed off to the side a tiny black and white puppy sort of shoved into the corner of the cage. He wasn't even half the size of his litter mates. I asked about him and Jane told me that his mom had rejected him, so she was just waiting for him to die. Now, even if you were really in fact waiting for the puppy to die, would you admit this to someone? And even if you hated dogs, if breeding puppies was your chosen vocation and you were concerned about trying to make some money, wouldn't you be feeding him yourself? Or trying to get one of the other hundred mama dogs to take him in? This was my first clue that something wasn't quite right with Jane. And also my first glimpse into her blackened soul.

I looked around at all the other pups…there were so many to see. I will spare you the details in regards to the conditions of the cages. And her website didn't lie. She had every possible color of dachshund you could imagine. But I kept going back to the little runt who had been rejected. He reminded me of something that had happened in my childhood, which was clearly foreshadowing into my life as an adult…I just didn't realize it at the time. Our family took a trip to Disneyland. There was this shop that sold nothing but stuffed animals. My dad told us that we could pick out any one that we wanted. Size or price didn't matter. The sky was the limit. So, squealing with delight, we all took off in different directions to find our perfect stuffed animal. My sister picked out a dog that had real fur and a radio inside (rabbit fur…gross, I know, but this was the 70's when rabbit fur was the thing). My little brother picked out a very large stuffed bear that was dressed in a suit and had a top hat. I had been scanning the shelves and one of the first things that caught my eye was this tiny stuffed dog named "Clem." I knew that was his name because he had a little nametag on. That was it, though. No clothes or fancy top hat. No radio. He was just a small little stuffed animal with very sad eyes and a plain white nametag. Nothing spectacular. Nothing special. I kept on looking. There were such elaborate things in that shop. Life-sized lions, animals that were puppets, animals dressed in costumes with sequins and feathers. Everything you could think of. But I couldn't get little Clem out of my mind. I was worried that nobody would buy him because he was so small and sad. I was concerned that nobody would think he was special and he would never have someone tuck him into bed at night. I lamented about this as only an eight year girl can. So, I went back and got him. I had "rescued" my first dog.

Okay, back to Jane and her dirty kitchen. I asked Jane if I could have the tiny, rejected puppy. She hesitated. I mean, if she was just waiting for him to die, why wouldn't she give him to me? Well, she said I could have him, but I would have to pay for him. So she actually did have the sense to know that I wasn't leaving there without a puppy, and if she gave him to me for free than I wouldn't buy one of the healthy puppies and then she wouldn't make any money. And her husband wouldn't like that. And judging by her black eye and missing teeth, keeping her husband happy seemed like a wise choice. Now, in hindsight, which we all know is supposed to be 20/20, I should have walked out her door and gotten into my car and driven straight to a hospital and had some sort of shock treatment that left me unable to remember the last twenty four hours of my life. But I didn't. I told Jane I would buy this little dog. And I did.

I left Jane's nasty trailer. I felt dirty. I felt like I needed to take a long shower in Clorox bleach. But I didn't only feel dirty on my skin, I felt dirty in my soul. Like, maybe I should go to confession...and I'm not even Catholic. Because beyond the foul odor that had attached itself to me from the trailer, I felt dirty knowing I had just paid the most evil woman in the world five hundred dollars for a dog that was feloniously neglected and on the verge of death. I just helped keep her in business. But I didn't have a lot of time to think about that right now. On the way home I bought puppy formula and made an appointment at the vet for the very next morning.

I named this tiny little dog Orville. Orville, as it turns out, was only five weeks old. I had paid a hundred dollars for each week of his life. He was dehydrated. He was weak. And he was all mine. Well, I had gotten him to be a friend for Peabody, but Peabody (who was suffering from a thyroid issue at this point) was a hefty twenty eight pounds. Orville was one and a half pounds. Not sure that is the recipe for good playmates. And my vet wasn't even sure

Orville would live. But he did. And he and Peabody wound up being pretty ambivalent about each other. Which, at least, was a step up from the Peabody/Folgers relationship. I still have Orville. He is blind, diabetic, has a bad heart and is really, really mean. And despite my best efforts, he doesn't have a friend in the world. And he's still all mine.

I think now that I must have had some sort of post-traumatic stress disorder after being at Jane's house. I couldn't stop thinking about it. I was sort of obsessed with it. I was pretty worried about what was going on over there. But, I decided the best thing to do was just try to forget about it. I had saved little Orville's life. That was enough.

Fast forward a year and a half. I had adopted another dog. This dog was from a dachshund rescue in Texas. His name was Seymour. He had been rescued from a puppy mill where he had been horribly abused. I felt good rescuing a dog from a puppy mill, mostly because of the way that the rescue volunteers would refer to the term "puppy mill" with such spite and disgust. When I adopted Seymour I didn't exactly know what a puppy mill was. I just knew that I was doing something good. I was doing the right thing. But after getting him, I did some research. Then it all clicked. Seymour hadn't been my first puppy mill rescue, Orville had.

If I had been obsessed before, now I was obsessed and psychotic. Jane ran a puppy mill. I started visiting her web site several times a day. I felt so angry. How could I have been so stupid? I mean, first of all, looking at her website, the only place that the photo of the "beautiful farm" she claimed to live in could possibly exist would be either Wisconsin or Oregon. There aren't any green, lush rolling hills like that in Texas. Secondly, she did 99 percent of her business online. You ordered a puppy and she had it shipped to you. I think I was probably one of the few people who actually got to see Jane's den of sin. She was charging thousands of dollars for puppies and her claim to fame was her unusual colors. She had an image to create and uphold. If people knew the truth of her situation, she would probably be stoned to death.

Then the unthinkable happened. I was on her site one day and I saw Orville's mom up for sale. That sweet little red and white dappled dachshund dog with the largest eyes I'd ever seen when I first walked in to Jane's kitchen. The happy one that was wagging her tail. Jane was selling her for three hundred dollars. She was eight years old. I was pretty worried about this. I wasn't sure what Jane would do to this dog if nobody bought her, but, knowing what I knew about puppy mills at this point, I had a feeling it wasn't going to be good.

So, yes, I went and bought her. I know that buying isn't the same as rescuing, but sometimes that is the only way to get the dog. And I was all about getting the dog. When I was there rescuing Orville's mom, Betsy, I saw Franny. Franny was a tiny dachshund so pregnant that her belly touched the ground. She was only six months old. I asked Jane Doe if Franny was for sale and she said, "I would never sell her, she is going to be my star breeder." Well, about a year later Jane Doe contacted me about Franny. She said that Franny had encountered a "problem" while giving birth. Jane, with all of her veterinary experience, which is none by the way, did her own major surgery on Franny right there on the dirty kitchen table in order to save the puppies. In Franny's case, this meant a C-section with a pocket knife and no anesthesia, then sewing her up with fishing line which caused, surprise of surprises, a very serious infection. Poor Franny was in really bad shape. But Jane saved the thousand dollar puppies, and that was all that mattered, really. Jane was calling to ask if I wanted to buy Franny. Otherwise, she was just going to have to "let her go." I asked Jane if I could rescue Franny as I happened to be volunteering for a dachshund rescue at that time. She said, "No. I don't let my dogs go into rescue. I don't want to get the reputation that my dogs need rescuing." In my personal experience at that time and now, over a decade later, Jane's dogs need rescuing more than any other dogs I've ever seen.

All of the adult dogs at Jane's house were like skeletons. Jane added grass clippings to what little kibble she did give them so as to "fill them up" without blowing the puppy profit margin. The dogs also had so many ear mites that there wasn't enough room in their ears for all of them, so they had overflowed and set up little Hooverville mite camps on the dog's heads and noses. So, yes, I bought Franny. Infection and all. I paid Jane three hundred dollars for the privilege of saving Franny and denying Jane the pleasure of bashing Franny's head in with a brick, and then paid my vet almost two thousand to cure Franny's infection.

I once asked Jane what she did with the dogs that she couldn't sell. She pointed to a large, round cylinder of a building that was on her property. Her own personal incinerator. Orville had always been afraid of the smell of food cooking, and now I knew why. When they had outgrown their usefulness, this is how Jane got rid of the evidence.

Franny wasn't the last dog I bought from Jane. The dachshund rescue I used to volunteer for would do fundraisers just so we could go out and "buy" dogs from horrible places like Jane's that refused to let their dogs be rescued.

Jane was an evil person and ran an evil operation. But one good thing did come of the whole thing. Since meeting Jane on that hot, humid day, I have devoted my life to dog rescue. When I saw all those old dogs that had been living at the puppy mill for their entire lives something happened to me. Sort of like when the Grinch's heart grows three times its normal size when he realizes the true meaning of Christmas. My heart grew that day with love for those old dogs. Jane made it crystal clear what my destiny was to be. And though I couldn't save all of the old, broken down dogs that Jane had, I still rescue in honor of them. I rescue in their memory. I do all I can to make sure that as many old dogs as possible will leave this world with a name that is theirs and theirs alone, a full belly, tons of unconditional love and the knowledge that they mattered and that they will be missed.

As for Jane, she is still alive. Apparently, the song is correct. Only the good die young. She no longer breeds dachshunds, she now breeds Siamese cats. So, if you've ever thought about starting a Siamese cat rescue, now would be the time. And when I find myself lying in bed, exhausted from worry, stressed out and overwhelmed by my work and yet still unable to fall asleep, instead of counting sheep I think about the plans for constructing a large round cylinder in my own backyard. It won't be for unwanted puppy mill dogs. Nope. It will be for the people who run the puppy mills. And Jane will be the first test subject. It still won't do justice for all of the pain and suffering that she has caused over the years, but at least I'll sleep a little better. Which would be good. Running a dog Sanctuary takes lots of energy.

The Legend of Walter

In the span of a little more than one year, my life changed dramatically and it had gotten really, really complicated. I had moved back to Colorado from Texas. I had a young son. I was recently divorced. I was moving to the mountains so I could have the proper zoning I needed to keep the dogs I had rescued in Texas. I had to get a job. I was getting remarried to someone I hadn't seen since High School.

I thought that I was busy before, but I had no idea that my life could have escalated into how busy it was now. I had been at my job for a month, enduring a three hour round-trip commute every day. I was juggling the eleven dachshunds, a toddler who didn't speak, my new husband who worked fourteen hour days had never lived with a woman before (let alone a woman with a mute toddler and eleven messed up dachshunds), and the usual chores that need to be done when you have a family. And the dogs were taking up a lot of time that I just didn't have to begin with, so something had to change. And, in my mind, the only change I could make was to not get any more dogs and just wait for the ones I have to die off and then I could just have a "normal" life like everyone else and maybe things wouldn't be so hectic all of the time. I hadn't yet realized that I was just not destined for normality.

15

So, with tremendous showmanship, I threw my arms up in the air and proclaimed, "I am not getting any more dogs!" I just wasn't. Everything had changed and I was moving on with my life. I had saved enough of them. I had done more than my share. Somebody else could pick up the slack. I didn't need the stress or complication of the dogs I had now, and I certainly didn't need the added stress or complication of any new ones coming in. I definitely had decided no more dogs. Then I saw a photo of Walter.

I was contacted by an old friend working at a shelter in Nebraska in regards to a very overweight dachshund named Romeo. His owner had decided to go on vacation and didn't have anyone to watch her dogs. So she dumped them both at the shelter. She then decided she could maybe take one dog on vacation with her, but not both. For some reason, two would be one too many. So she decided to leave Romeo. She said, "He is old and won't live much longer anyway. And by the way, all he eats is cottage cheese and hot dogs. He doesn't have any teeth, so I chew the hot dogs up for him before I feed him." This was the conversation with the staff as she left Romeo at the shelter. Really. I kid you not. You can't even make this stuff up. And if you could make it up, I don't know why you would.

Now, I know dachshunds are not supposed to be fat. I did dachshund rescue for many years and I had several paralyzed dogs, I knew the risks of an overweight dachshund. Yet, at the same time, my heart cannot resist a chubby dachshund. It just can't, I have no defense against it. So when I saw Romeo's picture for the first time, looking so plump and round that his belly touched the ground, there was no turning back. No saying no.

Sometimes I will call my husband and ask him for advice. I'll say, "I need your advice on something." He says the same thing every time, before I can say another word he says, "Just say no." But I couldn't say no. The Nancy Regan 1980's slogan didn't work for this. Romeo was old, abandoned and chubby. Besides, we were about to move into our new house, we had agricultural zoning, we could have another dog. And, I had been told he wasn't going to live long anyway. They suspected he had Cushing's disease. An advanced case of Cushing's disease, no less. All we were really providing for him was hospice care for a few months. "Well," I thought, "if it's only for a few months." This is one of the more popular excuses I use to talk myself into these things. It's rarely true, but it helps. And it works on Erik, too.

So, it was done. Romeo was coming from Nebraska. Two women had volunteered to drive him out to Colorado. My husband was to meet them in Castle Rock. Castle Rock is about an hour and a half away from our house, and this was the first time that Erik had gone on a run to meet someone transporting a dog from another state. And they were just passing through on their way to New Mexico. Erik was convinced that they would either be really, really early or really, really late. This sometimes happens with transports. But not in this case. Erik only had to wait for five minutes before the women showed up.

It was a beautiful spring day. Erik had parked just off the highway at an outlet mall, close to a small patch of grass. Erik was concerned about Romeo being over-active for the ride home, so he had brought a leash, a collar, and a dog kennel. He felt prepared. Ready for anything.

The women got out of their car. They reached into the back seat and pulled out a beach-ball of a dog. It was Walter. Well, his name was still Romeo at this point, but neither Erik nor I liked that name, so it wouldn't be Romeo for long. We typically rename our dogs. Especially if the dog is deaf or doesn't seem to answer to their name. We like to do away with their "slave names" (especially the puppy mill dogs) and give them a fresh start with a new name. However, sometimes we can't change their names because they know and actually answer to their name. A prime example would be Coco and Princess. Two elderly, unfortunately named poodles who aren't deaf and who actually know their names. Coco is a boy with a girl's name, so everyone refers to him as "she" and Princess is not sweet and dainty like a princess, she's a mean bully, so it is

17

confusing. Our chubby Walter looked nothing like a Romeo.
Walter was always just, well, Walter.

Anyway, the women (yes, it took both) put him on the ground
and he promptly fell over. And he just stayed there. And stayed
there. And stayed there. The two women were very upset from
having transported Walter. Apparently, every time that they
stopped to see if he had to go potty, this is all that would happen;
they would put him down and he would fall over. They were
convinced that he was too old and too sick to travel. It appeared to
them, with all of their wisdom and knowledge about dogs, that
Walter was on the verge of death. They were enraged that the
shelter was rehoming such a fragile dog. They believed the shelter
was being grossly negligent. They apologized profusely to Erik that
Walter may not even live long enough to make it to the Sanctuary.
Erik made the drive home without incident, Walter lying next to
him the whole time. No collar. No leash. No kennel. Welcome to
the world of bringing home an old dog.

I remember the first time I saw Walter. He could barely walk.
He would go two steps and then have to rest. His tongue hung out
the side of his mouth. He was indeed as rotund as his picture had
indicated. His front foot was smashed so he had a limp. I was in
love. He arrived just in time for dinner. After being carried up the
front steps (I couldn't tell who was more out of breath at this
point, Walter or my husband) I served him a bowl of dog food. He
didn't know what to make of it. For some reason he couldn't figure
out how to eat out of the bowl. He had been hand fed the pre-
chewed hotdogs in his previous home, so a bowl was a strange,
unfamiliar and entirely unwelcome addition to dinnertime. So was
the dog food. He looked at me like a toddler might look at you if
you served him a bowl of lima beans. I'm a pushover so I ran to
the fridge and made him a concoction of cheeses, lunchmeat and
tuna fish. This was more to his liking, but this bowl thing just
wasn't working out. Walter had this way of looking at you when he
disapproved of something. He would look down at the bowl and
then look back up at me like, "And what am I supposed to do with
this?" I agreed to hand feed him, but I was drawing the line at

chewing his food. Luckily, he didn't seem to have any issues chewing his food anyway. I was relieved. I mean, I could sort of see myself doing this for a dog, but I'm a vegetarian and Walter wasn't, so it wouldn't have worked. Erik would have to have done it. And I don't know if Erik would have shared.

Walter eventually learned that dog food wasn't too bad. In fact, I don't think there was anything Walter wouldn't eat. He loved eating dog poop. Being in a home with so many other dogs was like a dream come true for Walter. He could snack on dog poop all day long out in the back yard. And he also learned to eat out of a bowl in the kitchen. He was turning into a regular dog!

I have to admit, having Walter around was a joy. He was one of those dogs who just feel entitled to your love. Walter could've been shuffled around from owner to owner and he wouldn't have cared. He knew that everyone would love him, hand feed him and possibly chew his food for him. He wasn't one of those dogs that are fearful or shy. He wasn't depressed from being dumped by his owner. I don't know that I'd call him normal, but he was happy. He was just living in the moment and loving every bit of his life and he was thrilled to be here. He knew how good he had it. It is especially nice when that happens.

But it wasn't all wine and roses with Walter. We quickly discovered that he had a lot of issues that weren't initially disclosed to us. The first thing was that he walked with a limp. There was no mystery as to the reason for this. His front paw was flat. The pads on the bottom of that foot were all smashed together making one big strangely shaped pad. He was missing two toenails on that foot. His owner had told the shelter that his foot had been run over by a car. She said since he was old and wouldn't live much longer anyway, she didn't have it treated. She also said she didn't think it hurt him. Had she actually touched his foot, she would know that her assumption was completely and utterly wrong. It hurt. It hurt badly. But, other than amputation, there was nothing to be done at this point.

Walter also loved to bark. Almost as much as he liked to eat. When he barked, his whole fat body would pop off the ground. His front feet would get about an inch in the air and he kind of looked like a low-rider car bouncing up and down. And Walter was under the mistaken impression that he could jump. He'd be on the floor and try jumping on the couch. If he gave it all his energy and effort, his front feet might get two or three inches off the ground, but his massive hind end never budged. But he thought he was jumping and we admired his gumption. Instead of waiting for us to pick him up, he'd just try to jump over and over and over. I actually believe he thought he was actually going to make it on the couch one day. But he never did.

However, his main focus was food. I'd never met such a food-focused dog in my entire life. If he could eat 24/7, that was fine with him, and with us. He was old. He was going to die soon. He should at least be happy in the tiny amount of time he had left. So we gave him lots of food.

We feed the dogs twice a day. At 7:00 a.m. and then again at 5:00 p.m. We do this like clockwork. The dogs like having routine, and so do we. This way, we can monitor the feeding and see if someone is not eating, or eating too much. The schedule also helps us in administering medication. It is important that we have control.

Some dogs are okay eating around other dogs, and some need to eat by themselves. Some dogs won't eat if they think other dogs are watching. They would spend a month guarding the food in front of them instead of eating it just to make sure that nobody else got it. Walter had his own routine. He liked to eat in the middle of the hallway. We don't know why and we never tried to figure it out. As long as he was happy, we didn't care. With his bowl in the middle of the hallway, nobody tried to eat his food and he didn't bother to go to anywhere else to try to get anybody else's food. It took him a long time to eat, but he didn't care. And, again, we didn't care, either. We were happy because eating kept him quiet. It was one of the few times in the day that Walter wouldn't bark.

One evening, all of the other dogs were done eating and were either roaming around the house or sleeping and Walter was just about halfway done with his meal. Erik and I heard barking and looked down the hallway. We saw Walter eating, so it wasn't him doing the barking. We looked past Walter and into the bathroom. Orville was in the bathroom and he was barking at the toilet. As you remember, Orville is the tiny black and white dachshund I rescued from the horrible Texas puppy mill. I rescued Orville, his half-sister Zelda, who lives in a closet, and their mom, Betsy, who lives in a kitchen cabinet. Now, Orville would generally spend his time catching and eating flies and getting in to fights with other dogs. But he was not a barker.

We yelled at Orville to stop barking. While Walter was eating, there wasn't any barking in the house. This was our quiet time and Orville was ruining it. But Orville wouldn't stop barking. So I stepped over Walter and went in to the bathroom to see what was going on. And then I saw that Orville wasn't barking at the toilet at all. He was barking at what was behind the toilet. A baby chipmunk.

I yelled for Erik and he got a bucket and a large piece of cardboard. I don't know if these are the Martha Stewart recommended materials you are supposed to use to remove a baby chipmunk from your home, but it is all we had and the eviction was mandatory and needed to happen fast. I picked up Orville, who continued to bark, and put him out in the kitchen. I was sure that, given the chance, Orville would try to get a second meal if he could catch it.

Suddenly, the baby chipmunk ran out of the bathroom and in to the hallway. The baby chipmunk ran in circles around Walter. Walter kept eating. Erik ran in circles around Walter, chasing the chipmunk. Walter kept eating. I got on the other side of my husband and cut off the chipmunk. The chipmunk ran under Walter, hiding under Walter's belly fat. Walter kept eating. I picked up Walter and his food bowl. Erik put a bucket over the chipmunk. Walter kept eating. Erik put the cardboard under the bucket and picked the bucket up, capturing the chipmunk. I put Walter and the food bowl back down. Walter kept eating.

My husband, son and I ran out the front door and down the porch steps and out to the front yard. My husband put the bucket down. We were going to give Oliver a lesson in capturing a wild animal in your house and releasing back in to its natural habitat. Because, you know, it is the right thing to do. Erik released the baby chipmunk and it just stood there. And we stood there. And it just looked at us. So we decided that maybe it was just nervous because we were so close to it, so we walked back up the steps onto the porch to watch the glorious event from there. When we turned around, we saw the baby chipmunk. And we saw a red fox standing about five feet behind it. Erik and I rushed Oliver into the house and quietly shut the door. Walter started barking. He was done with dinner. And he had missed all of the excitement.

Now, fast forward two years into our life with Walter. He was fifteen when he arrived at the Sanctuary. He was now seventeen. He was only supposed to live a few months at the most. His blood results for the Cushing's test had somehow gotten lost but he had nearly every symptom for it and it should've killed him by now. Yet, he seemed to be getting younger. Spry and spritely instead of gangly and geriatric. Due to his new diet of actual dog food as opposed to pre-chewed hot dogs combined with the exercise he got from the hours he spent wandering the house and yard looking for more food, Walter had dropped lots of weight. Lots. He went from weighing twenty eight pounds down to a respectable seventeen. He actually looked like a normal dachshund. I didn't feel like I had to pretend I was pet sitting him for some crazy relative when we were in public. I was a proud mama.

And best of all, I didn't have to sit in the chair of shame and listen to a lecture when we went to the vet. And we went to the vet a lot. Walter in no way rivaled Peabody in the medical department, but he always had these strange illnesses. One time he lost a huge round patch of fur on his back. We took him to our regular vet and he couldn't diagnose it. We took him to a dermatologist, he gave us (well, gave isn't really the right word, more like traded for one hundred dollar bills) special creams, diets and shampoos. Nothing worked. But at least Walter smelled really good. Honestly, for the first year after we got him, I swear he smelled like hotdogs… mixed up meat and liquid smoke. It was nasty.

Finally, after developing a circle of missing hair the size of a dinner plate on his back, we went to another specialist who pretty much just threw his hands up in the air and prescribed Clavamox. Clavamox is for dogs what Penicillin is for people. An average generic antibiotic. Nothing special. Well, within a week the hair started growing back and he was cured. It was like giving somebody an Aspirin to cure a brain tumor, and then having it actually work. It was incredible.

Another time Walter stared vomiting. And vomiting and vomiting. And…vomiting. Having had several dogs who have almost died from pancreatitis, we were worried. We took him to our vet. After doing an examination, our vet said that Walter needed to go to the hospital. The dreaded emergency vet. The place with the flat screen televisions and espresso machine and the five hundred gallon saltwater fish tank in the lobby. The place where it costs two hundred bucks just to walk in the door. We drove him the forty five minutes to the hospital where he was admitted for fluids and tests. Nothing was conclusive. All they had to go on was the obvious. He was vomiting. Lots and lots of vomiting. That, and he was old. And I could have told them that, without the flat screen televisions, espresso machine and the impressive salt water fish set up.

We had to leave him there overnight. The house was so quiet without him. I couldn't sleep I was so worried. The next day we went to the hospital to visit him. I will never forget, it was Thanksgiving Day. My husband and I had been driving around all afternoon delivering food to people who couldn't afford Thanksgiving Dinner and wondering who was going to bring us Thanksgiving Dinner after we got done paying Walter's bill. We walked in and Erik drank three espressos (he always wants to get his monies worth) and the vet took us to the back ICU room where Walter was. She was telling us that they didn't really know what was wrong with him. I was looking over the "estimate" which was well over a thousand dollars at this point. I noticed they were giving him Tramadol. I asked her why she was giving Walter Tramadol for vomiting. The vet said that Walter's pain was so severe he wouldn't stop crying, so they were keeping him on pain meds. I asked her if they had been withholding food because of the vomiting. She said "of course." I suggested that she try feeding him to get him to stop crying. She put some food in a bowl and put it in Walter's cage. Walter's eyes got really big, he immediately stopped crying, and he ran over and ate the entire bowl. His pain was emotional. Psychologically he had convinced himself that he was starving to death. He rapidly improved after food was reintroduced into his life.

The next morning, we got a call from the vet that Walter could come home! He was eating well and no longer crying. And, no, they never did figure out what was wrong with him. In the end, we got to pay seventeen hundred dollars for a stomach ache. Yet it was still the best Thanksgiving I've ever had.

As a few more years went by Walter started developing a bit of dementia. Being a senior dog sanctuary we are pretty accustomed to dementia. Almost everybody comes down with it at some point if they live long enough. It is something of a badge of honor around here, it shows that you are living longer than anyone ever expected and perhaps longer than you would have really wanted. There are, however, varying degrees of the malady. Walter's dementia made it impossible for him to back-up. He just couldn't figure out how. He had one direction, and it was forward. He would get behind a door and stay that way until someone came to rescue him. Corners were bad, too. If a situation involved something more than forward he would just bark his head off until rescued. The only problem was that by this time he was deaf as well, so he barked nonstop anyway.

Everyone in the house was at Walter's beck and call. Sometimes he would be barking and I would ignore it, thinking it was his regular barking, only to go back an hour later and find him in some precarious situation. That made me feel horrible so I sort of lived my life following Walter around making sure he was okay. His other favorite activity was getting off the bed at night and barking. It was his hobby. I think he just wanted to test your commitment to him. Would you choose to try to sleep, or would your devotion to him get you out of bed every hour of the night to rescue him from being trapped in the corner, standing in the water dish, or being stuck under the nightstand? Erik and I always erred on the side of "better to be safe than sorry." It is inconvenient to be safe, but it can be heartbreaking to be sorry.

Walter lived to be twenty-one years old. Yep. The dog that barely survived his trip to Colorado and who was expected to expire within a few months of arrival lived with us for just over six years. And, as strange as it sounds, we miss his barking. Especially at Thanksgiving.

Green Acres

I've always wanted chickens. Always. Something about them is just fascinating and soothing all at the same time. The sounds they make, the way they scratch around in the dirt. It has been a life-long dream of mine which came true several years ago. My husband has also wanted them, but for different reasons. Practical reasons. Logical reasons. Technical reasons. Mostly for the eggs and compost. If I were into cooking and gardening at all I could probably see that side of it. But I'm not, so I didn't. Which is okay.

In our normal fashion, we got the chickens way before we got the coop. I don't think we've ever done anything in a sensible, logical order. I tend to make impulsive decisions and just hope it all works out. That is my style. My husband's style is to research something for so long that it never happens. He just researches it into oblivion. He doesn't ever make a decision about whether it is right or wrong, good or bad. He doesn't act on it, he just researches it. So, we have no middle ground over here. Decisions are either made suddenly without any thought, or they are not made at all. But my husband is always trying to make me happy, so if I talk about something long enough, he will act upon it.

Although, and certainly my husband included, who doesn't love the thought of baby chicks? I mean, I can't think of many things that are cuter and more wonderful than a baby chick. If someone is depressed, they should prescribe "farmaceuticals" instead of "pharmaceuticals." Give people a baby chick instead of an antidepressant. You simply cannot be depressed while you watch a baby chick go to sleep. They flop over mid-step like they've been struck by lightning. They are suspicious, curious, sweet and vulnerable; not to mention super-soft and super-fluffy. And the innocent, unsuspecting, unpretentious "Peep Peep Peep" sound they make is simply music to my ears. What's not to love?

Well, we weren't exactly sure how to go about this process. We looked at the larger hatcheries, but you had to get a minimum of twenty five of a specific breed. That was a problem. We only wanted about twenty total, and we wanted a bunch of different types. There are a few places where you can get just a few, but they are very expensive. We have feed stores near us that sell them, but they are just "chicks." They don't tell you what kind of chicks. Boys. Girls. Buff Orpington, Plymouth Rock or Rhode Island Red. Nobody knows.

Eventually, we found a place with a minimum order of twenty-five, but you could mix different sexes and breeds. The reason they make you get twenty five is that the chicks are shipped and they need to stay warm by using body heat. Now, I admit, I was pretty shocked to find out that they ship day old chicks. Seems like an awfully inhumane thing to do. I struggled with this, but wasn't sure how else to get them. The company assured us that they rarely have fatalities when shipping chicks. They wait until the weather is warm enough so they don't freeze and not too warm so they don't cook and you have to make sure your post office knows the chicks are coming so they can alert you so you can immediately go pick them up the moment that they arrive.

We didn't have any sort of chicken coop or chicken run or anything at this point, so we set up our chick nursery in the garage. It consisted of two dog pens put together with plastic cable ties, a ton of pine shavings, some heat lamps (chicks have to be kept very warm) food dishes and water stations. The space between the wire on the bottom of the wire pens are pretty wide, so we had to cut up eight inch tall pieces of cardboard and attach it all the way around so that the chicks couldn't slip out. Or, worse yet, so that a large mouse or wood rat couldn't slip in.

We kept boxes of baby wipes to make sure they didn't get pasted up and then waited for the big day. And, no, I didn't know what "pasted up" meant until a week before they arrived. But we had gone out and gotten several books on chickens, and we had been doing a lot of research online. Knowledge is power. So we were ready.

My husband got the call from the post office at about nine in the morning and drove to get them while I eagerly awaited their arrival. I went down to the garage. I set up some chairs around the pen. I had the hand sanitizer. I was ready to be blown away by "cute." Then came the phone call. Erik had opened the box and discovered that most of our chicks were dead. We only had five survivors out of twenty five. Now, if a baby chick is the best thing in the world, a dead baby chick is certainly the worst, let alone twenty dead baby chicks. My husband discretely removed the five that were still living and hid the carnage from me. Even though the baby chick company insists that they rarely have fatalities, they also warn you not to open the box in front of your children. They should extend that warning to people who rescue wild rats, relocate wasp nests and cry at the thought of a dead goldfish. Basically, they should have extended that warning to include me.

Well, in true Little Old Dog Sanctuary fashion, even though we had death and tragedy, there was no time to wallow in sadness or mourn. We still had five survivors to tend to and they were not going anywhere and they were hungry. Very, very hungry. Sitting in the chick pen with the babies was my idea of heaven. They are so tiny they feel like holding a cotton ball. They scurry around like the Armageddon is coming. I loved spending time with them. If I could've brought them into my bed, I would have. Meanwhile the company was sending in the replacement chicks, which didn't seem like a good idea after the last disaster, but they wouldn't refund our money, they would only replace what had died. Now, I completely understand looking back at the whole situation, that I shouldn't be supporting a company like this. It is like a puppy mill for chickens. But at the time I was clearly blinded by chick lust. It can happen to the best of us.

Unfortunately, in the week that had elapsed since we placed our order, the breeds of chickens that we wanted were no longer available. Yes, we were dealing with a large company, but they were still at the mercy of Mother Nature. If the chicks don't hatch, they can't sell them. So we stayed up late and studied the few breeds that were still available and we also decided that we should order a few extra…just in case. Now, a little side-bar here, a "few extra" in Sanctuary terminology means pretty much almost doubling our order. So we ordered forty. We had also ordered a rooster. Now, there is always a chance you'll unknowingly get a rooster in your mix. We were ordering pullets. Girls. They would grow in to hens. We could have ordered "straight run," which is "you get what you get," or we could have ordered roosters. Straight run should be 50 percent hens and 50 percent roosters, roosters are 100 percent roosters, but pullets are 90 percent hens with a default 10 percent "whoops" factor built in. So you have a 1 in 10 chance of getting a rooster when you order hens. But we had wanted a rooster. And what if we didn't accidently get one? We'd have to order twenty five more chicks. We were not having great luck so far, so we decided to hedge our bets and just order one. So we did. And they would be shipped in a week. And we didn't sleep for a week. That is how it went.

This time, my husband went down and talked to the Postmaster every day for a week. We were going to make sure that the moment the chicks landed at the airport, the Post Office would do everything they could to get the chicks out of the box as soon as possible. The company called us the afternoon that they were shipped out. We set our alarms (yes, we set several alarms) to wake us up extra early the next morning. I don't know if it actually helped to be so proactive at this point, but it felt good to be doing something.

My husband was at the Post Office at 7:00 a.m. the next morning as they unlocked the front door. The Postmaster saw my husband and immediately tracked the package. The Postmaster made two phone calls. It was determined that the shipment containing the chicks was fifty miles away at the sorting facility, just Northeast of Denver. It wasn't expected to arrive in our sleepy little mountain town until 3:00 p.m. Well, as you can expect, this was not acceptable. So the Postmaster got in her truck and drove down to get them. My husband came home ate breakfast and took a quick power nap. I didn't eat, I didn't take a power nap. I just worried.

Two hours later, my husband was back at the Post Office. He waited for the Postmaster in the parking lot. She pulled in. My husband took the box and opened it up. It was full of chicks, and they were all alive! And, as we soon determined, the chick company had also thrown in some extra chicks as an attempt to appease our broken hearts. There were a total of forty-seven chicks, and not a single fatality.

I thought that five chicks was heaven, but fifty two baby chicks is about as near to paradise as you can get. I wanted to sleep with them at night. I would sit in the pen with them and they would crawl all over me. They loved to peck at my clothing, my toenail polish, my hair. I had to teach them to eat and to drink. We put marbles in the saucers that contained their drinking water so they wouldn't fall in and drown. They would sleep in chick clusters under the heat lamps. Then they started to grow. When they are just a few days old, they sort of all look the same. Sure, some are darker and some are lighter, but they all look the same. Then, they change. Dramatically.

Well, if you have ever had chickens in a confined space you know about the chicken dust. And if you have not lived through it, you would almost not believe it. The magnitude is overwhelming. I had not prepared myself for such a thing. And chicks (as well as chickens) are messy. I would clean their water about seventy five times a day. As soon as I put a fresh watering station down,

someone would run over and poop in it. They step in their poop,
they run through their food, they fling wood chips everywhere and
they scratch the floor, presumably searching for food and grit.
Now, I guess you hear old-timey tales about chickens scratching
but when they are doing it in a confined space you really get to see
what exactly that means. They make so much dust. Our garage
looked as though we were recreating Oklahoma, circa 1934. Yes,
we were re-living the dustbowl.

Suddenly, one morning, we went out and realized that the pen
was crowded with teenage chicks. Really. It happens in the blink of
an eye. It was sad they were so large, my fluffy little powder puffs.
But they were also healthy and thriving so we were doing our job in
raising them correctly, and I knew that, at some point, they would
have to grow up. They were still cute. But you couldn't hold five of
them in your hands. You could hold one. Sort of.

It was about this time when I decided the chickens might like
some fresh air so I set up a pen in the front yard where we have
this tiny patch of grass. I envisioned them loving the grass, the feel
of the breeze, the sunshine on their feathers. Not quite so. They all
froze. They were like chicken statues. They didn't want their feet
on the grass. They wanted back in the dusty garage.

At this point they were all trying to figure out how to roost.
They were all sitting on the top of the pen instead of inside the
pen. We would occasionally have one that got out of the pen. Now,
our garage is like something from an episode of Hoarders, so losing
a chicken in that can be quite the problem. We didn't want to be
cleaning out the garage in a year and discover a petrified chicken
carcass. These chickens needed to move out of their parent's
basement and get a place of their own. It was time.

While I had been spending my time indulging in chick love,
my husband was frantically building them a run and then we were
going to hire someone to build a coop. I warned my husband that
if he didn't build the run secure enough and if something happened
to one of the chickens, I would hold him fully responsible. Their
little fluffy lives were in his hands. So, like any good husband who

is afraid of the wrath of his wife, my husband built a run that rivals Ft. Knox. He used 200 feet of heavy-gage, six foot metal fencing inside our already fenced in area (affectionately known as the "big yard," which is a thousand feet of fencing.) He made the run so our Great Pyrenees could completely encircle it, protecting the chickens. It has a double entry way just in case someone slips out the gate from the coop, they won't be able to get out in to the big yard. They would still be contained.

Erik risked his health and welfare chopping off, or "topping," the tops of the pine trees inside the run so he could put aviary netting over the entire top of the run so nothing could slip in through the top. This was probably the most dangerous part of the whole endeavor. I mean, an exhausted, slightly overweight, middle aged man with no balance and a bad back standing on the top step of a six foot ladder on the side of a hill using a chain saw with a fresh blade…what could go wrong? Well, at one point, the chain did fall off the saw and slap him in the chest, and another time he slid down the ladder and tore his hands up on the tree, but, in reality, considering what could have gone wrong, he was pretty lucky. Nothing was going to stop this project.

Besides sinking the fencing into the ground, my husband, the researcher, also discovered a way to keep out predators that sounded logical and seemed to have great success. Erik was only able to sink the fencing a little bit because our land is very, very rocky. So he had to lay down a piece of fencing horizontally beneath the vertical piece and attach them together. He used tiny bits of wire. With the amount of complaining he did, and the number of cuts he had on his hands, it looked like it was not an easy chore. Then he covered the horizontal piece of fencing with dirt, rocks and tree trunks. This keeps animals from being able to burrow their way under. This was all great. But we still had no coop.

We hired some men off of Craigslist who built the coop in two days. They were awesome. My husband is pretty good with fencing, but his fine carpentry skills leave a little to be desired. The coop has some beautiful windows that we had gotten the previous summer at garage sales, and it is insulated and level and waterproof. It has the big door in the front for people, and the little door on the side (inside the main chicken run) for the chickens. Perfect! So we were set.

The only problem now was, well, me. See, I don't like change. I was worried about the chickens being outside. I was worried they would be too cold (though it was August by this point, and even though we live in the mountains, it gets pretty darn warm in August.) I was worried they would be scared. When really I was just anxious and I love to place my anxiety on others. It took me weeks to build up the courage to take them outside to their new home. We finally did it on a very sunny day in September. We had to do a few at a time in a dog carrier. All my worries were for nothing because they loved it. And at dusk they all made it into the coop on their own, without any coaxing from us. Just like the books and magazine articles said they would.

The days and weeks passed and we noticed we had two roosters. One beautiful exotic naked neck rooster we named Ezra and one mean little Speckled Sussex rooster we named Cornelius. We were very worried about the two fighting. Everything we'd ever read said you can't have two roosters. But one thing I did read in a single, obscure magazine article that I have never seen since, was that if you add a goat into the mix the roosters won't fight. I had never heard of such a thing. I talked with some people who had lived on farms, and Erik talked with some people who had lived on farms, and they had also never heard of such a thing. But, they also said that it seemed logical. The roosters, wanting to be the alpha grand overlord of the barnyard, see the goat as being the alpha. So they don't even bother to fight and they just give up and live their lives in peace. And, this gave us a good reason to get goats, so I was all on board.

I rushed to find some goats before we might discover that Cornelius and Ezra weren't ever going to fight and my cunning plan for more (and different!) animals would be foiled. We drove a million miles to the middle of nowhere to a place that had two goats they wanted to rehome. These were baby pygmy goats. There was a girl and a boy. We named them Petunia and Gus. They were about the cutest things in the world, but very afraid of everything. Us, the chickens, rain, sunshine, the dark, clouds, Tuesdays. You know. Everything.

Gus had been castrated and dehorned. Petunia had only been dehorned because goats can't be spayed. Now, we were happy to know that Gus couldn't participate in making babies, but not as thrilled to discover that he has lost his only means of defending himself. The same goes for Petunia and her lack of horns. I mean, they have them for a reason. We became even less thrilled when we found out that Gus had actually died during the dehorning procedure. They gave him a whopping dose of adrenaline directly into his heart and brought him back to life. Apparently, this is a common occurrence with goats during this procedure. They do castrating and dehorning without anesthesia or pain meds, so, really, if you ask me, dying doesn't seem like such a bad choice. Ultimately, Erik built a couple of pens inside the coop, and we housed the goats separately from the chickens. At night, at least. During the day, everybody all lives together. All was well with our little farm.

Then one day we found an egg. Now, this may seem strange to you, but I hadn't really given thought to the eggs. I don't eat eggs, I don't like eggs. But suddenly here they were, eggs. Don't get me wrong, it is pretty exciting to see your first egg that isn't in a carton that you buy from the store. It was, more or less, the typical "egg" shape, but not perfectly white. We have brown eggs, white eggs, blue eggs and green eggs. They are beautiful. They come in strange sizes and variations at times.

But after you get over the quaint loveliness of having your own eggs you have to figure out what to do with them. We tried feeding them to our dogs, but old dogs are similar to old people and have very delicate digestive systems and the eggs proved way too wholesome for them. Every once in a while, we get a severely malnourished dog that tolerates eggs and the eggs will literally save their life. But even if the eggs only make a few of our dogs sick, if even one of those dogs gets an egg, it can be a messy situation. Not to mention dangerous, if they get dehydrated from having such bad diarrhea. And, unfortunately, the dogs that don't react well to the eggs never remember that they don't react well to them. Eggs and the dogs are like my husband and a dozen donuts. Just because you can eat them doesn't mean you should eat them. And I certainly wasn't about to eat an egg. No way.

So we started plying all of our friends, family, acquaintances and complete strangers with eggs. I have been told we have the best eggs that people have ever tasted. I tell them that is because our chickens are living a stress free life. I don't eat eggs, so I certainly wouldn't eat a chicken. The chickens seem to know this and they appreciate it. So out of gratitude, they lay golden eggs we have no use for. And never will.

At this point I thought we were settling in to our little farm nicely. The chickens were happy, we had no losses, and nothing had been able to get into the coop. The little goats were growing a bit (fatter, not taller) and life was good. That was until one day I went into the chicken run and Cornelius tried to kill me. Up to this point Cornelius had never really paid much attention to me. But suddenly I was his arch enemy. I came in that day covered in blood from the long scratches and deep puncture wounds from his huge spurs. Now Cornelius was sort of a scrawny rooster. We had many hens larger than Cornelius and they would constantly beat up on him. The hens would pick all of his tail feathers out. Ezra was giant and beautiful and the hens loved him. Cornelius was mad and jealous. Really, really mad and jealous. Naturally he did what any bully would do, he decided to pick on someone he thought he could beat up, which I guess was me. I was getting seriously wounded out there. I started having to carry around a water bottle so I could spray him in the face if he tried to attack me. Sometimes this worked and sometimes he just didn't care.

I know, most people would have gotten rid of him in one way or another. I knew if I tried to "rehome" him he would become fricassee. I didn't have the heart to do this to him. He was just being a rooster, after all. So I just learned to arm myself. I had to dress in appropriate clothing he couldn't tear through on his first attempt. I couldn't go inside the coop unless I shut him out in the run first. He had figured out that he could get in the coop up on a roost and jump on my head while I was collecting eggs. I started wearing glasses and a hat. He still gets me sometimes, but we both know this is just the relationship we are destined to have. He gets to attack me and show off in front of the ladies, and I get to go inside and disinfect my wounds. And so it goes with life in the barnyard.

Worst Purse Dogs...EVER!

If I had to do it all over again, I would run a Chihuahua rescue. I've had experience with dozens of breeds of dogs, but Chihuahuas are by far my favorite. And they are very misunderstood. When I hear the term "Purse Dog," it makes my stomach churn. Popularized by celebrities, Chihuahuas are touted as an accessory rather than a living entity. They are a product, simply existing so they can be shown off and attract attention. And then they wind up as an afterthought rather than a life-long commitment. Sure, when they are puppies, tiny little innocent babies, they are sweet and beautiful and precious. But babies grow up. Vlad the Impaler was probably a cute baby, but he wasn't so cute when he grew up. The same can generally be said of Chihuahuas. They just don't age well.

Chihuahuas are the second most over-represented dogs in shelters, right behind the Pit Bull. In every piece of literature I've read about them, they are not recommended for households with small children because of how easily they are provoked. Really. They are psychotically aggressive. A 2009 study using Colorado Veterinary Medical Association data shows that Chihuahuas are the most likely breed to bite their vets. The Chihuahua's teeth are fine and sharp, which allow for greater penetration and greater damage to nerves and tendons. In theory, this makes the dog's bite more painful. I don't know if the bite is more painful, but they seem to bite more often. We've only had one dog that has ever bitten Oliver, and it was a Chihuahua. Or, as Oliver prefers to call them, Chick-a-wa-wa's.

Chihuahuas, or Chick-a-wa-wa's, are an acquired taste. Definitely not for everyone, for sure. But I love them. They are intense. They are full of love, they are full of hate, and they are fully unique. But they don't make good fashion accessories. I have three examples that support my belief.

The first one is Claude. He had the markings of a Rottweiler. A seven pound Rottweiler. And he had this massive, barrel chest and thick neck and broad shoulders and a tiny waist and little, stubby, miniature legs. He looked like a body builder who spent way too much time working on his upper body while ignoring the fact he had a stomach or appendages. When he first met the other dogs, it was obvious that he was an alpha. If anyone or anything was in his way, he moved them out of his way with his thick neck and shoulders. He wasn't aggressive about it, though. He would just walk through them, sort of like the Incredible Hulk would walk through a wall. When we got him, his name was Piglet. Well, all I could think of was that Piglet from Winnie the Pooh would be far too meek to act like this, so I really wasn't liking his name. At all. But the actions of our fearless little Piglet reminded Erik of one of his favorite hockey players of all time, Claude Lemieux. Claude was generally regarded as a ferocious player and spent a lot of time fighting, but he is also one of only ten players to win the Stanley Cup with three different teams (or so I'm told). Our little Claude was ferocious. And it turns out that our little Claude was also a Champion. A Champion hoarder.

That's right. Claude's favorite occupation was hoarding. And he was the best we've ever seen, too. It didn't matter what the object was. It didn't matter if somebody else had it, or if he just found it out laying in the middle of the yard. It was always an adventure to look in his little bed to see what you would find. Sometimes it would be another dog's favorite toy. Sometimes it would be a pinecone. Or a rock. Or poop. Or a ball of fuzz. Or a piece of paper. Or car keys. Or a plastic milk jug lid. Or sometimes all of these, and more, at the same time. He wasn't picky, but he was determined and relentless. Like he had a quota to fill or something. He would proudly acquire the object of his desire and hide it in his bed. He would have been an excellent candidate for an intervention.

And it was always easy to know when Claude was guarding something. He had a terrible poker face. His body language was always the same, no matter what, except for his eyes. He had two looks. His eyes were either scanning the room for something to take, or his eyes were scanning the room to determine who he had to defend his precious bounty from. It was during his guarding periods that there would be a fire emanating from his pupils that would telegraph, "Stay back. I am willing to die for this half-chewed pine cone with the splotch of bird poop on it. You wanna' try me, punk? Do 'ya?" Well, nobody every "tried him" because nobody ever wanted his junk. But one dog's junk is another dog's treasure. And Claude always thought he had a treasure.

One of the best things to watch, ever, in the history of the Sanctuary, was Claude when he would be running at full speed and try to go around a corner. It wouldn't matter what the flooring was...wood, carpet, tile, whatever. But as soon as he would try to make the turn, his legs would drop out from beneath him, he would roll anywhere from four to six times while perfectly executing a 90 degree turn, then land right back on his feet and continue to run just like nothing out of the ordinary had happened. It was like he planned it all along. He performed this physical comedy routine daily.

It was possible that Claude could have made it as a purse dog, but not in the traditional sense. I don't think he would mind going in to the purse, as long as there was a lot of stuff in there that he could hoard and guard. But the problem would be that I don't think he would ever want to come out. And if you tried to reach in and get your lipstick, well, say goodbye to your thumb.

Claude eventually died from heart failure, but he lived life to the fullest. Bold, brash, beautiful and mentally ill enough to be willing to fight to the death over a pine cone taken from a yard that has 10,000 pine cones that all look exactly the same. We never thought we would ever have a dog that could top Claude's eccentric personality.

But, as the old saying goes, never say never. Enter...Flora.

Flora was older than Claude when she arrived, and she only lived a meager four months before she died...also of heart failure. But we focus on quality of life over quantity of life, so she certainly had a happy four months here. She had a sour face, but a sweet heart. She was also a riddle wrapped in an enigma encapsulated by a quandary surrounded by the opening credits of the original Twilight Zone. She had a lot going on and kept us entertained, to say the least.

I had gotten a call from a county shelter that they had an eighteen-year-old Chihuahua needing a home. Well, when I went to pick her up the staff noticed she looked rather fat...all belly, and after a brief exam by a tech, they concluded she may be pregnant. Actually, the tech was quite convinced that she was pregnant. Hmmm. An eighteen year old Chihuahua that was pregnant. I'm not a certified vet tech, but I had my doubts. Besides, regardless of what was going on with her, I was taking her home, so it really didn't matter.

She seemed healthy and alert at the shelter, and we were at the shelter longer than usual because the staff was trying to rummage up what little they had to offer me in the form of whelping supplies, but about halfway home she started coughing. It was obviously kennel cough. And then she started sneezing. And then she started dispersing this green snot slime all over the place. On the seat. The dashboard. The car door. It was somewhat reminiscent of The Exorcist. We have a lot of The Exorcist moments at the Sanctuary, but I have never, ever seen a dog become so ill from kennel cough. So now I have a maybe/maybe not pregnant dog with the worst case of kennel cough in the history of canines. Lovely.

The next day, after a visit to our regular vet up by our house, it was determined that Flora had a brutal case of kennel cough and she needed to be quarantined in my craft room. Which she hated. We had to give her IV fluids twice a day and antibiotic shots three times a day. This did not thrill her. Or us, for that matter. A quarantine situation at the Sanctuary is designed to be relaxed, quiet and contained. The dog is usually doped up on pain meds and recovering from surgery. The dog wants to be away from other dogs. The dog is happy to be left alone. The dog wants to sleep and not be disturbed in any way. But not Flora.

When she wasn't running from us to avoid being poked by a needle, she'd stick her head through the baby gate and get stuck. And it would be one of those typical "child's head caught in the banister call the fire department" sort of situations. This happened multiple times until Erik finally rigged solid objects between the railings. But since she could no longer see us, this would just upset her even more. She so wanted to be around people. And we so wanted her to be happy. It was a sad situation for all of us.

I'm not sure what Flora's past was like, but she was found living in the parking lot of a convenience store. She was a feisty, scrappy thing. Her fur was rough like AstroTurf and turns out what was once thought to be a belly full of puppies was really just Cushing's Disease. And she had a bad heart murmur. She was missing huge patches of her AstroTurf fur and what she did have was sparse to say the least. This caused her skin to get these half inch to one inch long "rips and tears." The skin would just sort of split open for no apparent reason, then scab over fairly quickly and heal up while other parts of skin tore open. But this was not any more disgusting and gross that the usual disgusting and gross stuff that we deal with on a daily basis. That not only says a lot about her life and what she had to endure, but is a good metaphor for the Sanctuary. The Sanctuary is a living unit that sometimes splits apart at the seams, heals, splits, heals, and, through it all, carries on. And you are brave. Even when you don't feel like being brave. If Flora was ever in any pain, she never showed it. And she introduced us to a new style…a style she wore very well. It was not a style befitting of a purse dog. It was more like Dumpster Chic. And she had it mastered.

After a few weeks, her cough settled down. She went in to the general population and quickly assimilated herself. She became the "grand dame" of the upstairs room. She was the self-proclaimed matriarch of all beasts with four legs and was not to be messed with. Even though she was mostly deaf, she could feel and would respond to vibration. One day, Erik was sitting at the computer trying to get work done and Wilkie (a particularly obnoxious Chihuahua who Erik absolutely despises) was doing his usual routine of barking really, really loudly at absolutely nothing. I mean, he could have been barking at something, like a mysterious and invisible energy field or ghosts or something like that, but none of the other dogs could see them and therefore nobody else cared, so it just came off as Wilkie being a loud, obnoxious jerk. Erik was yelling at Wilkie like he always does and Wilkie was ignoring Erik like he always does. Flora got up from her pillow, walked all the way across the room, and grabbed Wilkie by the neck. Erik stopped yelling. The dogs that were licking their paws stopped licking. The dogs that were napping woke up. The room was dead silent. All eyes were on Flora and Wilkie. Even the blind ones.

Just like everyone else in the room, Wilkie was dumbfounded. Wilkie's eyes got really big and he stopped barking. Wilkie was not in any pain…just pure, unadulterated, absolute shock. Flora let go of Wilkie's neck and walked back to her pillow and laid down and curled up and went back to sleep. Wilkie just stood there for a few minutes, then went and hid under a blanket. Soon, all was back to normal. But from that moment on, all of the "upstairs" dogs sure knew who was in charge.

But that was not Flora's most memorable event at the Sanctuary. Not by a long shot.

Now, I pride myself in being a responsible dog owner. And, as a responsible dog owner, it is only logical to be prepared. I was looking at the dogs one day and thought about one of the worst possible scenarios that a dog owner can fall into. Having a lost dog. It occurred to me that I had photos of most of the dogs, but not all of them. I thought about how I would feel if I lost a dog that I didn't have a photo of and had to canvass the neighborhood with Lost Dog posters? So I began my mission of getting photos of each and every dog. But the journey to get photos of all the dogs would only prove one thing, that no good deed goes unpunished.

When I had my sudden epiphany, Flora was a recent addition to our pack and we didn't have any pictures of her, so she was at the top of the list. Well, one cloudy Saturday morning we got out the camera and started taking some pictures. We had to use the flash on the camera because it was so cloudy. Flora didn't much like having her picture taken and wasn't being cooperative, so we gave up on her, took some pictures of other dogs, and went about our day. A few hours later I noticed I hadn't seen Flora in quite some time and started looking around. Nothing. I started to panic a bit. Our son, who was four years old, had been upstairs by himself for a brief period of time, and when I asked him if he had opened the front door he said no. Then he said maybe he had. Then he said he did and he thought he saw Flora walking down the driveway. And then he said he saw her get into a car and they drove away. But maybe not. If you've ever tried getting really important information from a four-year-old you'll know exactly the frustration I was feeling at the time.

But Oliver cast a shadow of a doubt and we still couldn't find her, so I thought she had gotten outside. It was April, and we live in the mountains. The days were warm enough but the nights were still brutally cold and Flora hardly had any fur, was mostly blind, deaf, and pretty much had none of the attributes that you would need to survive in the wilds of the Rocky Mountains. And since she couldn't hear, there was no calling her name and having her come to you. And I knew she had come into the shelter as a stray, so wandering off on her own wasn't anything new to Flora. She was fearless.

I quickly called the shelter to ask who her microchip was registered to, and found out she had not been micro chipped. They only microchip dogs who are being adopted, and I was just "permanently fostering" Flora because she couldn't be spayed because of her bad heart. And we don't keep collars on the little inside dogs because there is too much for them to accidently strangle themselves on when they are in the house.

Well, luckily, or so I thought at the time, I had the picture of her! After a few hours of looking we made up some LOST DOG signs. I have to tell you I felt like the lowest, crappiest pet owner in the universe making those signs. "LOST DOG: Eighteen year old Chihuahua, deaf, mostly blind, ten pounds, Cushing's disease, needs meds." Who had I become? We posted these signs everywhere. We took turns outside looking for her (she was, of course, the color of the brush up here in early spring so she would blend right in) and there is so much land to cover. It was a needle in the haystack situation.

When night came on and it started to get cold I couldn't even function anymore. I thought of her out there with her tiny bit of ineffective fur, she hadn't eaten dinner, she needed her meds, she wouldn't know where she was or where she should go, and she was just the perfect size for a nice fox snack. It was the worst night of my life. My husband spent most of the night looking for her. My only hope was that someone had stopped and picked her up and would see our signs and contact us. That felt like the longest night in history.

The next morning I went downstairs through our mudroom to the garage. I noticed a dog had pooped and peed on the floor down there and just assumed it had been a dog from the night before. I asked my husband about it when he got up and he said there hadn't been any dogs down there. The mudroom is just a tiny room full of closed boxes. I had looked for her down there the day before. We had searched the whole house a dozen times. We knew if she was in the house she would come out for dinner, she always knew when it was time for dinner. Well, my husband went down again and checked the mudroom for the thirteenth time and guess who jumped out of a box (with a lid on it) and rambled up the stairs? As relieved as we were to find her, we were also concerned by her decision to relocate and isolate herself. One of the behaviors common to our dogs, right before they die, is that they will find a new, out of the way place to sleep and spend their final days. Or day. Or hour. But this wasn't actually the case for Flora. She lived, quite happily, for another two months. It was the flash from the camera that sent her over the edge.

And that is why she would have made an abysmal purse dog. Imagine a celebrity walking down the red carpet on their way to see the world premiere of their new movie. The movie star fans and the paparazzi are all lined up, eight deep, behind red velvet stanchions, waiting for that "perfect picture." Little Flora pokes her little head out of the top of the eight hundred dollar purse and suddenly three hundred flash cameras all go off at once. Poor Little Flora would spontaneously combust. And that would not make for a pretty picture. Except for maybe in The National Enquirer.

Last but certainly not least in the list of awful purse dogs, we come to Chico. Chico is a Chihuahua who came from New Mexico. His owner got involuntarily placed in a nursing home, and Chico got involuntarily placed in a high kill shelter. I was contacted and informed that Chico was in desperate need of a home. Immediately. Today. And that transportation to Denver had already been arranged. And, as a matter of fact, they had already been driving all morning and would be in Denver in an hour. So, certainly, with the added element of his owner being forcibly placed in a home, I was happy to have Chico be a part of the Sanctuary. My husband works close to downtown, but he was also scheduled to go and pick up a load of baby chicks several hours to the south of Denver. If anything, he and Chico were going to get some road-trip time in.

This was all very sudden and I didn't even get to see a photo of him. All I was told about Chico was that he is old. Very, very old. And that he was going to be killed at the shelter because he was so old. And, yes, Erik and I would agree, Chico is old.

But, strangely, they forgot to mention a few rather obvious facts about Chico that were impossible to overlook. Upon my husband meeting Chico and his transport on a street-corner downtown, there was a little bit more going on with Chico besides his age. One of his eyes was in really bad shape. Goopy, mostly closed, white, abnormally small. And he was born without a tail. We thought that maybe he lost his tail at some point, or it was docked for some reason, but there was no scar and no remnants of cartilage or bone. He also didn't have any teeth and his tongue constantly stuck out of his mouth. Now, this sort of thing we were used to. But something else also stuck out all of the time. His penis. This, we were not used to.

Chico was happy to be handed off to Erik and go on another road trip to get baby chicks. He had just traveled for six hours, and he had another five ahead of him before he would set eyes, or eye, on the Sanctuary. Chico slept peacefully on the floor for the entire drive. His ears perked up at the sound of the chicks, but other than that, Chico didn't care what was going on. Erik pulled over halfway through the trip next to a stretch of grass and tried to get Chico to go potty, but all Chico wanted to do was get back in the car. So he did.

Erik called me when he was about half an hour away from the house and we both agreed that Chico had a lot of stuff going on with him, but the trade-off is that at least he seemed to be a really mellow dog. We love it when we get a mellow dog. They are few and far between. And when they are mellow, it makes our lives easier. Even if just by a little bit. And we appreciate that.

Erik pulled in the driveway. Within seconds of entering our home, Chico violently and relentlessly attacked and bit my son Oliver. We would soon discover that Chico would violently and relentlessly attack and bite all men who would come in the house.

Well, except for Erik, who wasn't thrilled to be categorized as "not a man." Generally, when a dog bites you and he doesn't have any teeth, essentially snapping at you with his gums, it doesn't hurt. But not so with Chico. His gums are, somehow, really sharp. It wasn't long before Chico would attack the other dogs. And sometimes even toys. But never Erik. So much for a mellow dog.

Chico was underweight, just like most of the dogs when they arrive here. But after an expensive surgery to remove his little eye, Chico started feeling better and was eating more and was quickly on his way to becoming comfortable, content, and portly. And he still likes to fight. But he also discovered that he likes to sleep. So at least he isn't fighting all the time. Just most of it. I guess he figured out that if he wants to fight so much, he'd better make sure he gets plenty of rest.

After a consultation with our regular vet, it was confirmed that, yes, there really is nothing we can do about his dangling penis. So we had a semi-violent, overweight, one eyed, genital-exposing dog without teeth or a tail. But the real kicker was that we had Chico for almost a month before we discovered that he only understands Spanish. We thought he was ignoring us. But it turns out we were just being poor hosts. Chico is now bi-lingual. And now, to a certain degree, so are we.

Chico is still as feisty as the day he arrived, and may actually make a good purse dog. But not for just anybody. He would probably only work out for a masochistic, kinky, Mexican pirate porn star.

In an honest attempt to provide full disclosure, we have had a few purse dogs at the Sanctuary. And we even have a couple of them right now. But they are considered purse dogs not because they are fashionable or adorable accessories, but because they can't walk, and a purse is a really convenient and practical way to move them around. And they love it.

Moby Dick Times 10,000

I got my first aquarium when I was about seven years old. I remember going to these Girl Scout Fairs where one of the games was that you reached into this plastic pool filled with sand and rocks. If you picked up a rock and it had a fish drawn on the bottom of it, you won a fish! I always pulled a rock with a fish on it. I thought I was just so lucky, but, thinking back on this, I now realize every rock probably had a fish on it.

I couldn't imagine a better prize than a goldfish! I would come home with these goldfish much to my mom's dismay. We just put them in a bowl as that seemed to be the standard gold fish habitat back then, but they would die after a few days. I would be hysterical. I think my mom tired of this hysteria I would exhibit every time a fish would die, as well as the subsequent overly-dramatic funerals that followed, so we got an actual aquarium for the fish so they might live more than a few days. I remember getting lots of regular goldfish, calico goldfish and those black goldfish with the big eyes. Those were, and still are, my favorite fish. I would watch that aquarium for hours.

In my adult life I decided I wanted another aquarium. My husband had a piranha, but I was against this. Well, I was happy that he had a pet. And I guess at this point in my husband's life (he got this fish when he was a bachelor) a fish was about all he could handle. I mean, when you're single with no wife or kids, have a really good job so that you actually have some disposable income and on top of it you can sleep twelve hours a day, the commitment of anything more than a fish would be daunting, wouldn't it? And if you spend four months researching the fish, one month naming it (and settling for, of all things, "Amazon" spelled backwards) and then two weeks waiting for it to arrive, well, I mean, really, how could he ever have the time or desire to care for a perfectly healthy and normal dog? Or, more specifically, the time to care for a bunch of old, sick dogs? Well, luckily, that is something you can marry into. But the biggest issue I had with the piranha was that I couldn't see having a pet that you had to feed other pets to. It just didn't make sense why this big fish's life was more important than the feeder fish's life.

Having another aquarium while we had the piranha (Nozama) didn't make sense. I mean we had another aquarium, it was for the feeder fish. I have blocked this time period out of my mind because taking the fish from one aquarium to feed them to a fish in another aquarium was more than I could handle. Nozama didn't live long after my husband and I moved in together. Only about a month. Erik is convinced I killed him and I could see how I would be the number one suspect. But I didn't kill him. I'd be the first to admit I thought about it, but how do you kill a piranha? Smother him with a pillow and dump him back in the tank? Entice him to eat a poisoned goldfish? Replace his water with really cheap vodka? All of these are doable, but none of them are believable as "accidents."

After Nozama died I had him cremated as a gift to Erik. I can hear you, right now, saying "Why in the world would you go and do something like that?" The answer is simple. I had not been caring, empathetic or even remotely nice when Erik told me that Nozama was dead. I just said something like, "It is just a fish." This from the mouth of a girl who would hysterically shriek and cry for days when her goldfish died. Plus, I guess I was confused why he didn't care about the trail of tears he led those feeder goldfish down for years and years. But, it was insensitive of me and I wanted to make it up to him. We had Nozama in a Ziploc baggie in the freezer. I called around and found a crematorium that would pick up Nozama and cremate him and return the ashes to me. I arranged to have the person from the crematorium come to my workplace to pick up the fish (as I was keeping it as a surprise for Erik).

I'll never forget that day. This man walked solemnly into my office. He was middle-aged and had a very strange vibe. I mean, I'm not the kind of person who is afraid of people and I don't judge, but this guy gave me the creeps. Even though he was dressed in a suit and acting very formal, I could easily picture him on his couch in his parent's basement, wearing a Star Trek snuggie, hair unwashed for days, South Park re-runs blaring on the TV while he lays passed out in a pool of stagnant bong water. Not impressive.

He sat down in my office acting very somber and shook my hand and told me he was sorry for my loss. Then he asked if I had the "deceased." When he said that, I laughed out loud. I know it was rude, but I couldn't help it. I had the "deceased" in the freezer at work. I had left a group message to everyone in my office about Nozama being in the freezer, lest he end up as some intern's fish sandwich during lunch. I retrieved the "deceased" and gave him to this strange guy. The freezer at work didn't really function very well so Nozama was defrosting and sort of limp and squishy. The strange guy pulled black gloves out of his coat pocket before taking the deceased. He wrapped him in an elaborate fashion and put him in a special box. A special, government approved, sterile and fully securable corpse transporting device. Okay. Not really. It was a Tupperware. And two hours before, it was probably holding his lunch.

He assured me he would take proper care of the deceased and that I could pick up his cremains in a few days. As he was telling me this, he told me that it would probably be best if I came alone to pick him up. I wasn't sure why he said this. Then he told me that when I came to the crematorium, it would be better if I parked in the alley and came to the back door. Alone. He actually said "alone" again. By this time I was pretty freaked out. I mean the hair on the back of my neck was standing on end. I could imagine myself going to pick up Nozama alone, parking in the alley and coming in the back door alone. Nobody would know I was there since it was a surprise for my husband (which, of course, I had told this gentleman) and I was alone. And it is a crematorium. Now, I watch crime shows on television. There are a lot of far-fetched stories of people who "disappear" because of really elaborate and drawn out and complex murder plots that people spend months and years trying to execute. Well, this would be neither far-fetched nor elaborate. As a matter of fact, it would be easy-peasy. Anyway, after a brief conversation with the voice in my head (in which the voice kept yelling "Danger! Danger!") I ended up telling my husband about the surprise and made him go pick up the fish ashes so I wouldn't be murdered. And, yes, the crematorium was at the very end of a bunch of industrial buildings in a rough part of town, and, yes, the entirety of the office was draped in black silk, and, yes, my husband wound up being extremely happy that I made him go and pick Nozama up instead of going by myself.

Anyway, after my husband spent a week grieving, we decided to get a real aquarium with fish that ate fish food (I know, I know, fish food is probably just ground up, dried feeder fish but it isn't me doing the grinding or drying, so I can deal with it). Now, my husband loves anything extreme, tacky, crazy or rare. He wasn't going to go for the goldfish, he wanted some strange exotic fish. Instead of going to the local Petsmart, we went to a real fish store. We bought two Parrot Fish for about forty dollars each. They were sweet and shy and beautiful. So what did we decide to get as a tank mate for them? Who were going to be their best friends in the whole, wide world? Something called a "Terror Fish" and two Jack Dempsey's. Again, we didn't research anything, we just got what we thought looked cool. We judged a book by the cover. Now the Terror Fish was tiny, and the Parrot Fish were huge so we were actually worried for the little fish. Imagine, being worried about something called a "Terror Fish." This fish lived up to his name.

He terrorized everyone in that tank. Even the Jack Dempsey's, which didn't turn out to be so nice, either. The Parrot Fish that we had dropped forty dollars each on we never even saw. They stayed hidden in the decorative "cave" in the tank lest they be murdered by the Terror Fish. The Terror Fish ate the fins off of the Jack Dempsey's. Not exactly the serene nostalgic tank I had dreamed of. The Parrot Fish both died of fright and I ended up taking the Terror Fish to my tiny fish tank on my desk at work. There was nobody to terrorize, so he died as well. We gave away the two mean Jacks. The fish tank, having been the killing ground for so many feeder fish over the years only to be quickly turned in to a container of horror and abject fear for the Parrot Fish, was promptly dismantled so as to cause no more harm.

Well, my memory is short and my nostalgia is strong, so we began looking for another tank about a month later. I wanted something huge. I wanted to watch tons of tiny fish swimming in schools. I wanted to hear the bubbling of the filter and I wanted harmony. I wanted regular fish that didn't stalk and try to kill each other. My husband, who is my alter-ego buzz-kill with his views of "realistic" and "if we stop and think about this for a minute," brought up the economics of the situation. Fish tanks are much more expensive than they appear on the surface. Besides the tank, you need a tank stand (to hold the weight, as water is very heavy,) a hood (with lights, of course,) a heater (or two,) a filtration system (or two,) gravel, decorations, food, and also cleaning equipment. Not to mention that the electric bill is going to go up. However, just as my husband is very good at bringing me back down to earth with his practical thinking, he is equally as good at doing my irrational bidding. Only a few days later, he found me a one hundred and fifty gallon tank on Craigslist for a steal! Buying real estate for fish is just like buying real estate for people, besides the location, it is all in the timing. Erik found some people who were leaving town in a day and were desperate to unload their entire set up. Erik was able to meet my irrational wants in a practical manner. It was perfect.

So, I had the biggest tank of my life and what did I proceed to do? I bought the tiniest fish I had ever seen. I don't even know what they were called. No, I didn't research them…why would you even ask such a thing? We are talking about me. Hope. Not Erik. All I knew is they weren't called "Terror Fish" and they didn't have shady, back-alley fighter kind of names like Jack Dempsey. They were tiny and friendly (that is what the card on the tank at the pet store said) and that is all I cared about. I think they were called "tiny unicorn rainbow love fish." It takes a lot of tiny fish to fill up a hundred and fifty gallon tank. So we started with about thirty. I was in love with them. I watched them all the time. Our tank was beautiful. But one day I noticed something. A tiny, tiny, super-tiny fish. A baby! I freaked out. I had no idea what to do. But we are taught from a young age that the "big fish eat the little ones," so I knew I just couldn't turn a blind eye and ignore the situation.

Erik and I spent hours trying to catch the baby in a net so we could put him in a very small, plastic compartment separate from the other fish. This plastic compartment was one of the accessories that was included with the tank. "Convenience" or "foreshadowing?" Both answers are correct. The worst part was that since he was so fast and so small, it took us about three hours to catch him. Where had he come from? How had this happened? I knew about the birds and the bees, but I thought that fish laid eggs.

Well, it turns out I had bought thirty live bearing fish and they were having babies. Lots and lots and lots of babies. At first we tried to catch them all, but it was a losing battle. Then we read that, yes, they would get eaten and not to worry about it. This kept me awake at night. I didn't like the thought of babies being used for food. I was right back in the place I was with Erik's piranha, and that made me pretty upset. Maybe my angst was projected into the universe, or maybe it was because I have a general tendency to overfeed all of my animals, but the babies didn't get eaten. Well, maybe a few of them, but none that I had noticed. For the most part, they grew. They were strange combinations of the fish we had originally purchased, assorted Mollies and Guppies that morphed in to one, "Muppies." Soon, we had well over sixty fish in that tank. Everybody was breeding. It was the tank of love – the Woodstock of the aquarium world. And as it happens at our house, nobody was dying. Everyone was living on and on and on. Pretty soon we must've had hundreds and hundreds of fish in that tank. It was starting to look like a feeder tank at the pet store.

The tank was getting terribly dirty, terribly quickly. Suffice to say that the situation was…terrible. At this time we were both working full time and nobody wanted to clean the hundred and fifty gallon fish tank with 10,000 fish. Most of the time there was so much algae on it you couldn't see the fish procreating. We went into a deep state of denial. I mean, what can you do? My plots to kill Erik's piranha could work on one large fish, but a gazillion little ones? No way. The only idea I had was to scoop them out by the bucket full and flush them down the toilet. And it would still take days, if not weeks, to accomplish this task. And then there was the lifetime of guilt that would immediately follow.

I soon concluded that if Craigslist had helped get me into all of this, then Craigslist could help me get out of it. After looking at hundreds of posts, I finally found a guy that rescues fish. I kid you not. "The Fish Rescuer." So we gave him a call. He would happily take our zillion fish off of our hands. He spoke to me in a kind, yet somewhat condescending voice. This wasn't the first time someone had made a poor choice of fish. He spoke to me about fish like I speak to people about puppy mills. It was a kind, yet stern lecture. But, really, if all I had to do was listen to the lecture and it would remedy the nightmare I was living, well, that trade-off was just fine with me.

So the fish went into five gallon buckets and we covered them with plastic which was secured with over-sized rubber bands. My husband met the fish rescuer in the parking lot of a convenience store at midnight. Yes, the fish rescuer had a part time job, and he worked the late evening shift. No, it can never be easy. Needless to say, we dismantled the fish tank, which was now known as the tank of "sex and shame," and sold it. We had learned our lesson, again.

Years have passed. I now work full time at home and feel as though I can really handle the responsibility of an aquarium. I mean it this time. Really. You should have seen the look on my husband's face. He turned a shade of pale that I would presume a ghost would turn after seeing another ghost. I could almost hear my husband crying inside. And guess what I got this year for Mother's Day? But this time, I'm sticking with goldfish.

Quoth the Raven

I got an email from a friend of mine at one of the county shelters. Is it sad that all of my "friends" work at shelters? Anyway, she said they had this very old terrier come in as a stray. She was discovered in the middle of a corn field. This terrier reminded her of her own dog who had recently passed away, so she had named her Angel. Would I please bring her to the sanctuary? I said, "Of course," and went to get her. I mean, her name is Angel. How could I say no?

The first thing I remember about Angel when I first saw her was her crazy hair. She looked like she had been electrocuted and then sprayed with a can of Extra Super-Hold Aqua Net in the middle of a Class Five hurricane. She looked psycho crazy. But I've learned, especially with dogs, you can't judge a book by its cover. I mean, you may see a Rottweiler or Pit Bull and think they look mean and intimidating and they turn out to be the sweetest babies in the world. You may see a tiny adorable Chihuahua with big, sad, watery eyes and it tries to bite your face off. Looks are quite deceiving in the animal world. A volunteer was carrying her and Angel licked the volunteer's face and we all sighed and cooed about how sweet she was! See, she looked crazy but she was just a sweet old grandma of a dog. She looked very old. She was blind and seemed deaf, too. She was a poor sweet old gal. No wonder they named her Angel.

I was told I should probably put her in a crate to transport her home. I typically don't do this because the dogs usually just want to lay in my lap on the freedom ride. But they said she might be too scared, so I put her in a small crate in the passenger's seat with the front of the crate facing me so I could see her. It hadn't been difficult getting her in the crate. She was very well behaved. The volunteers waved goodbye and the shelter staff thanked me and blew kisses to Angel as I drove away.

Typically, on the freedom ride from the shelter, the dogs are either very anxious (shaking and looking very nervous), terribly excited because they are happy (bouncing all around the car wagging their tails and barking and licking me), or they are so relieved that they immediately fall asleep. Angel did none of these things. She just sat there. And she seemed sort of, well, how do I put this? She seemed pissed off. I tried talking "baby talk" with her. That usually gets a reaction. But I got nothing. I figured maybe she's just deaf. I tried getting her to interact with me by reaching out and trying to pet her, but she did not care for that. In fact, I could feel hostility radiating out of the crate. She just glared at me the whole drive home. I kept trying to "make contact" with her, but now, whenever I put my fingers close to the cage, she tried to bite them off. What had happened to the sweet Angel who had kissed the volunteer at the shelter? How could her personality have changed so quickly? I decided it must be the crate. She didn't hate me. Oh no. That wasn't possible. All dogs love me. It is just a law of nature. She hated being in the crate. I mean, it's only logical. Who wouldn't hate being in a crate? And she probably has some really negative association with crates that psychologically damaged her. I have several dogs like that. "She'll be okay. She'll come around," I said to myself about a hundred times on the way home. Things would be fine once I get her out of the crate. So I just gave up trying to make friends with her and I drove home. But I have to admit that I drove a little bit faster than usual.

Now, it's always a bit dicey when we introduce a new dog to the pack. It makes me anxious. I never know exactly how everyone will react. But, one way or another, it usually works out and it's always fun to see who the new dog will bond with. And it's especially satisfying to see them make new friends. So when we got home I did my usual routine of carrying the crate up the steps and dragging it in the house and putting it on the living room floor and opening the door and then the dog is supposed to come out and see its new home. But this time, when I opened the door to the crate, nothing happened. Well, technically, something did happen. She refused to come out. She didn't retreat further back into the crate, and she didn't move forward. She did nothing at all. I figured if she hated the crate so much she would be dying to get out, but she wouldn't budge. So there went the theory of "it's not me, it's the crate." Darn. I tried pulling her out and she tried biting my arm off. I tried dumping her out, but she got her feet wedged in just the right place to hold herself in. This had never happened before. Ever.

"Well," I thought, "maybe she is just scared." She didn't seem scared but some dogs are a hard read. I decided to leave her in the crate with the door open and let her come out when she was more comfortable. I set up an X-pen around her so that nobody would bother her. Hours went by and she didn't exit the crate. She seemed perfectly satisfied spending the rest of her life just standing there...glaring a palpable hatred out towards the world in front of her.

Finally, after almost four hours, Angel came out of the crate and stood in the X-pen. I had her separated from the other dogs, but she couldn't live this way forever. It's just not practical at the Sanctuary. So I decided to bring one of the calmer dogs into her space to meet her. I brought up Champ. Champ is this strange looking sort of medium sized wooly mammoth mutt. He is about seventeen years old, has a liver the size of a watermelon and is about the most non-threatening, non-aggressive dog I can even imagine. He is very friendly and just wants to eat. If you reach down to pet him, he opens his mouth like a baby bird waiting to be fed. He makes what we call his "lovey noises" when he eats. It is a vocal expression of pure happiness. Well, Champ "met" Angel and his tail started wagging at a million miles an hour. Angel "met" Champ and immediately tried to kill him. Champ was done wagging his tail and he was ready to go back down to the kitchen. Angel didn't want anyone or anything within two feet of her. She was seething. You could actually see it - the seething. It rose in waves, just like heat off of asphalt in a 120 degree Death Valley summer swelter. Angel slunk around the house, bristling with rage, and then laid down in the middle of the kitchen floor, curled up and went to sleep.

When Erik got home I tried to prepare him for Angel. I told him how she kissed the volunteer. I told him she might need some time to adjust. He went over to meet her and when he reached down to pet her she immediately woke up and started snapping like a piranha at a steak. Luckily, she was mostly blind and had bad aim. She didn't ever actually connect with Erik to inflict any injury, but she sure tried. We didn't exactly know what to do with her. We decided maybe if we just left her alone for a while she would come around. Sometimes dogs need an adjustment period. It turns out Angel's adjustment period was the rest of her life, but how were we to know? Erik had his own take on Angel, whom he re-named Lenore. Erik never really gets to re-name the dogs, but he suggested this and it turns out he was spot-on. He took the name from the Edgar Allan Poe poem, The Raven. He wanted to name her after a character from Children of the Corn, but even though Vicky is tied to a cross with barbed wire, with her eyes ripped out and her mouth stuffed with corn husks, the imagery didn't quite do Angel justice. Honestly, it was far too tame. Besides, the old gal embodied all the haunting and evil that Edgar Allen Poe loved to write about and it was classic and timeless. Like her. So Lenore was the perfect name.

Erik thought that Lenore was the textbook example of what dogs were a long, long time ago. On the grand timeline in the history of earth, in the way, way, way B.C. of time, pretty much right after the last T-Rex tipped over and died and prehistoric man appeared, Lenore sprang from the horrifying depths of the underworld to be a companion for prehistoric man until said man was able to figure out how to make fire and fend for himself. Sort of a pre-fire companion, if you will. And, at that time and under those circumstances, the primitive species known as "Lenore" performed quite admirably. All at once being vicious, wicked, heartless, barbarous, soulless, ferocious, harsh and cold. However, in today's modern era where people want a pet that is "loving" and "caring" and "pleasant," the species known as Lenore just doesn't fit in. She isn't bad or wrong, as much as she was born about 20,000 years too late. Or, perhaps, she had been alive too long. If she would let us touch her, we could perhaps trim one of her toenails and have it carbon-dated. But she never let us touch her, so we never got the opportunity.

That first night we had her we did find one thing she liked. She liked to eat. She tolerated us giving her a bowl of food, but just barely. Then she did what she would do every evening for the rest of her life. She curled up on the bare floor in the exact middle of the kitchen floor and spewed an angry vibe. We tried putting her on blankets, pillows or soft beds, but she acted like we were trying to kill her. We tried putting her in other, more comfortable places in our house, she ended up right back in the middle of the kitchen floor. After having her several months, occasionally she might lay on a towel. But it couldn't be folded. It had to be flat, thin and thread bare. No Egyptian cotton for her.

During her "settling in period" Lenore wasn't changing much other than getting meaner. She loathed all the other dogs and hated to be touched. Luckily she was mostly blind and not as strong as Peanut (our resident evil dog) so she didn't do much damage. If you picked her up around the middle she would thrash around like a toxic fish trying to bite your hands and arms or, well, anything she could get her teeth on.

Despite her nasty temperament, we learned to love Lenore. Yeah, we're suckers. But she also had a vulnerability about her. She had obviously had a hard life. She didn't understand love, kisses or soft beds. She always seemed surprised and shocked that a meal appeared before her twice a day. And she also learned that there were treats to be had. Lenore knew one thing up to this point, hands weren't good. It took some time to get her to stop trying to bite us and bite the treat we were handing her instead. But we loved her, so we kept working with her. And it turns out that we weren't the only ones who fell in love with Lenore.

The mystery of Lenore deepened one night. Erik was up late doing paperwork, which is often the case. And, as is also often the case, he had to go out to his car which is parked in the driveway to get a folder of papers. He opened the front door and right there, standing on our cheesy but effective and practical "Wipe Your Paws!" doormat, was a young red fox. Erik looked down at the fox. The fox looked up at Erik. The fox started to walk in to the house. Erik slammed the front door.

Now, the glass on the front door is frosted, so Erik walked around the corner and into the kitchen so he could look through the curtains of the floor-length window and out onto the porch and have a direct view of the front door. The fox was sitting patiently on the "Wipe Your Paws!" doormat, waiting to come in. Erik tried to get the fox's attention by tapping on the window, but he got no reaction. So Erik just went about his business, doing one or two of the millions of chores we have to do every day.

About an hour later, Erik looked out the kitchen window and saw that the fox was gone. He really needed those papers from his car, so he went out the front door and on to the porch and started to walk down the porch steps. He looked down, and coming up the porch steps was the fox. Erik ran back in to the house and got the door shut just moments before the fox got in. Erik walked around and looked out the kitchen window and, again, the fox was sitting on the doormat, waiting to come in. Erik watched the fox for a few more minutes, then just gave up and went to bed.

The next night, the exact same thing happened. Erik needed to go out to his car, and was prevented from doing so by a fox who wanted to come in the house. The only difference this time was that Erik gave up sooner and was able to get more sleep.

On the third night, Erik opened the front door, just a crack, and didn't see the fox. Erik opened the door and went out on to the porch. He saw the fox. The fox was sitting at the floor-length window...staring into the kitchen. Erik saw that the curtains were up on the window, and he saw exactly what the fox was staring at. It was Lenore. She was sleeping, curled up as she always does, on the bare kitchen floor. Erik went out to his car and came back in the house. The fox didn't move. He was totally focused on Lenore. Erik was pretty wierded out by this. But what was even creepier was that this went on for one full week. At some point in the night, Erik would see the fox sitting at the window, staring in at Lenore. And his gaze was so precise, so intense, so focused, that the deck could have been on fire and the fox wouldn't have noticed. But what Erik, and I, found especially disturbing was that we could have a house full of dogs, including two of the best guard dogs a family could ever wish for, and none of them ever noticed a fox staring in the window, for hours on end, at the slumbering Lenore.

Obviously, we were wondering what the fox was up to. Did he think that Lenore was his mother? Or great-great-great-great grandmother? Did he love her? Did he hate her? Did he want to eat her? Kill her? Carry her back to Hell?

The fox is a powerful image in literature and in folklore, and foxes mean a lot of different things in different cultures. To Erik and myself, here at the Sanctuary, a fox was simply something that you didn't want getting in the hen house. In China, a fox sighting was thought to be a signal from the spirits of the deceased. The Celts would rely on the fox as their guide through the spirit world. In Japan, the fox symbolizes longevity and protection from evil. But we live in Colorado, and in Native American lore, especially with the Plains tribes, the fox is viewed as an entity that is luring one to their demise.

Ten days after the initial fox sighting, we awoke one morning to find Lenore in her usual curled up position on the bare kitchen floor, dead. Except for the lack of a pulse, she looked no different than she did every morning when she was alive. But her aura was different. Or maybe it was the void left by her aura. But the room had a feeling of peace.

Erik waited and watched for the fox every night for the next month, but he never came back. The Lenore/Fox connection has never been solved, and it probably never will be. But I think it's only fitting to take some liberty with the last few lines of Edgar Allan Poe's most famous poem and end the story of Lenore with…"and her shadow on the floor shall be lifted – nevermore!"

The Tramp and the Tramp

For most of my adult life, I had to wake up early and hurry to get ready and rush out the door, fight heavy traffic, blizzards and bad drivers just so I could go to be underappreciated and underpaid eight hours a day, five days a week, and sometimes on Saturday. Now I just stay home where I am underappreciated, not paid at all and I get to work twenty four hours a day, seven days a week and I'm about a million times happier and much more satisfied. Anyway, at one point, I had a somewhat traditional job working in a crappy part of town in an office complex that was probably state of the art in 1977, but now it was thirty five years later and it didn't look so great. The company I worked for was on the first floor in one of the three large, matching buildings. Above us on the second floor was a call center. You know, one of those places that hires people to call you when you are in the middle of dinner or are just about to finally have some quality time with your family. I don't necessarily have anything against the industry, and I am happy that people have jobs. But the call center seemed to attract and employ people who were, obviously, not thrilled to be working there. They were young, angry, reeking of cigarette smoke, cheap booze and marijuana. And, for some reason, even though it was a telephone call center, they had a strict dress code.

64

You could always tell when it was "break time" at the call center. The courtyard of our office complex was suddenly full of young people wearing cheap polyester suits and very short, tight dresses, smoking cigarettes and sipping Smirnoff out of their plastic Big Gulp cups. It was like having a rave in front of the building every day at 10:00 a.m., noon, 2:00 p.m. and 4:00 p.m. You could also be guaranteed to get a contact high while walking down the stairs in the parking garage. And that was back before pot was legal here in Colorado. I'm assuming now they are probably growing it in the elevator. Long story short, everyone who worked in the call center was really high for a place where the morale was so low. And I was always grateful that my life's path never took me that direction.

One freezing January day during the lunch break, on a total fluke, I just happen to be out front of the building having a ten second conversation with a co-worker before she left for the day. It was cold, and I hate the cold. It was lunchtime, and I always spend my lunch break in my office. The odds of my being out there at all were incredibly slim. Suddenly, I saw this tiny white blur dash across the busy street in front of the buildings…Colorado Boulevard. If you are from Denver and have ever been on Colorado Boulevard during the lunch hour, or any other time, you will understand how amazing it is that this little white blur of a shaggy dog didn't get hit by at least a hundred cars and killed. In my five year tenure at this company, several people have gotten struck and killed in the crosswalk when they had the little green "walk" symbol and had the right of way. Many more have been killed while jaywalking. This little dog dodged death at least a dozen times in fifteen seconds just by blazing across the street, and then it happened to run right into the courtyard of my office complex. The odds of my witnessing any of this were staggering. I probably had a better chance of winning the lottery. Yet, here I was. The universe was coming into alignment.

Of course, to see a little white dog made my heart leap. Not just because I like to rescue little dogs and here was one right in front of me in obvious need of assistance, but because of a strange situation that had been going on with my son. At this time, Oliver was four years old and was not at all talkative. When he did talk, he spouted out strange sayings and obscure references. Oliver didn't say a word until he was three years old, and from about ages three to five, trying to decipher and comprehend what he was saying was like transcribing an ancient, dead language from a culture that you didn't even know existed. Really. It was almost impossible. Anyway, a few weeks before this incident, I was driving Oliver to pre-school and he suddenly blurted out that I would be getting a new dog. I didn't think much about it. I mean, it doesn't take a genius to know that at some point I would be getting a new dog. I run a rescue. Getting dogs is what I do. But then Oliver told me it would be an old dog and it would be white and it would really, really need my help. Since Oliver never spoke, when he did, you listened. And he was always right. Erik was constantly trying to get Oliver to pick the winning lotto numbers or help him with his Fantasy Football team draft, but Oliver didn't care about any of that stuff, so he never did. This frustrated Erik, but there was nothing he could do.

I had been waiting about a week for a call from the shelter asking me to take a little white dog, but the call never came. When I saw this little white dog dashing across Colorado Boulevard and into the courtyard, I actually felt a little light-headed with the feeling of "this is supposed to happen!" Now recently the building management had just installed a little pond with a waterfall in the middle of the courtyard, surrounded by concrete benches, and they seemed to have spared all expense. It was a fairly craptacular effort. I guess they were trying to make the place more serene and add an element of class and an air of sophistication. In my opinion the money would have actually been better spent on hiring a full time security guard. But...whatever. At least the fountain gave everyone in the courtyard a good place to extinguish whatever it was they happened to be smoking, and the benches were so uncomfortable that nobody really loitered too long.

Not influenced by the serene water installation, the little white dog was absolutely frantic and scared to death. He looked like he was going to run right through the courtyard, but as he passed the serenity pond, this idiotic call center guy who was the only person stupid enough to be sitting on one of the freezing concrete benches threw his Big Gulp cup at him. The cup, which I would see in a moment was half-full of ice, hit the dog and the poor little guy fell into the pond. The serenity pond instantly transformed into pure chaos. When the little white dog was able to jump out, he ran off across the side street and then I lost sight of him. I was so angry. I mean, who does this? I ran up to the animal abusing loser and confronted him. He had a couple of tattoos on his face and reeked of stale cigarettes and alcohol and obviously wasn't a very nice guy by his actions and was probably a bit unstable, but I didn't care. He could see I was really angry, but he just called me a stupid bitch and walked away with all of the other call center people. Their break was over. I was going to follow him up to the second floor, but I knew that I had a much more pressing issue to deal with.

I ran inside to my office and gathered up my assistant and several interns and put them all immediately on the hunt for this dog. I was scared to death. This dog was wet. He was tiny. It was January in Colorado. I didn't think he would survive the night if we didn't find him. He would either freeze to death or make that dart back across Colorado Boulevard and get run over. I went to the parking garage to get my car so I could canvass the nearby neighborhoods. I called Erik in tears and in a complete panic. I told him about the dog and how it had fallen in the pond and was now going to freeze to death. Erik was trying to calm me down and I told him, "but you don't understand...the dog is white." That stopped Erik in his tracks. He knew that this was not just a dog, but Oliver's prophecy. Erik wanted to come down and help me look, but I worked an hour from home and he had to take care of the dogs at the house. Dinner and medication time was quickly approaching.

My team and I searched for almost two hours. It was getting dark and starting to snow and I was really upset. Then one of the interns called me. She had found him. He was hiding underneath a dumpster in the alley behind the Taco Bell. She was able to catch him and she brought him to me. He was a tiny thing and he was soaking wet. His fur was long and scraggly and he looked older, but not ancient by any means. Luckily, there was a vet's office right across the street, so I popped in and told them the sad story. They gave him a quick warm bath and cut some of the mats out of his fur.

I brought this scared little guy home and, boy, he was scared. He was (and still is) one of the most nervous dogs I've ever seen. He was shaking nonstop and darting around like a lunatic. He didn't want anybody reaching for him, touching him or really even looking in his general direction. I couldn't stop thinking about how Oliver's prophecy had come true. I mean, what are the chances that this dog would be at my house after all that had gone on earlier in the day. Ninety nine days out of a hundred I would not have been in the courtyard and I would have missed the entire event. Then Oliver came home and I said, "Here he is sweetie, the white dog you were talking about." Oliver took a fast glance at this dog and very matter-of-factly said, "That isn't the white dog. The white dog that is coming can't walk." Then Oliver turned around and walked up to the living room and turned on Finding Nemo for the billionth time. I was shocked. Not by Oliver's abrupt actions, but because I was wrong.

Doing a bit of research, I quickly learned more about this dog. This little dog was easily identified as a Maltese and, unlike most of the dogs at the Sanctuary, he conformed extremely well to the breed standard. The Maltese is a highly desirable breed and you rarely see them in shelters. You mostly see them on covers of magazines, groomed to the hilt, looking beautiful, delicate and perfect. They are expensive purebred dogs, and you don't see them for sale too often in Colorado unless it's at a pet shop. Someone had to be looking for this guy. So I guess he wasn't my white dog after all. Feeling deflated, I went about making "found dog" signs to hang up the next day.

I made forty copies of the sign and put them everywhere. A full week went by, and...nothing. Nobody seemed to be looking for a little Maltese. I was following up with a friend of mine who works at a shelter about another of the dogs that recently came to live at the Sanctuary and we got on the topic of the Maltese. She told me a story about a puppy mill in Nebraska that had been busted a few weeks ago. A puppy mill that was breeding Pomeranians and Maltese. There were so many dogs that they had to ship some of them to shelters in other states. Then she said that one of the volunteer transport vans was driving through Denver on its way to a shelter when it was in an accident. Several of the dogs had managed to get away, and many were still missing. My white dog had to be one of these dogs. And that was the end of that mystery. But the Oliver inspired mystery remained.

It is important to note that I've never had a Maltese before. I don't much go for the fancy dogs. I love Chihuahuas, Dachshunds…you know, little dogs that don't have this never-ending, somewhat expensive and generally inconvenient "grooming" thing going on. I mean, you wipe down a Chihuahua once a month with a wetnap and you're good to go. A Maltese? Nope.

First of all, they are white. Or, I should say, they are supposed to be white. And it takes a lot of effort with bathing and drying and brushing to make that happen. Secondly they have this very fine fur that is really more like a toddler's hair and it knots up and it's not easy to work with. Imagine you are trying to untangle a grumpy toddler's hair…a grumpy toddler who has sharp teeth. But, sadly, his behavior while being groomed closely related to his regular, everyday behavior. This dog was so traumatized I couldn't imagine rehoming him. So he was here to stay, even if he wasn't the dog Oliver said was coming. We named him Nigel.

Here at the Sanctuary we have little "gangs" not unlike prison. It is usually breed specific, again, not unlike prison. The Chihuahuas hang together. The dachshunds stick with other dachshunds. Then there is a group of the outcasts - this consists of the mutts, the occasional poodle and a terrier or two. Some dogs are loners and don't belong to a gang. But not Nigel. He is really

69

street smart. Nigel assimilated rather quickly into the Chihuahua gang. That was wise. He may have done it because Chihuahuas can be extremely violent, so he knew that he would be safe. Or maybe it was because Nigel could relate to their high strung shaking and annoying barking. So Nigel spent his days and nights curled up with several small Chihuahuas, shaking and barking. Barking and shaking. And being really, really happy.

Nigel loves to bark. He barks at anything and everything. He even barks at himself barking. I'm not sure why people love Maltese dogs so much. All they do is bark. And then they bark some more. And then you have to brush them. Fifty times a day. While they are barking. I am not used to this. We generally don't have a lot of barking at the Sanctuary (unless someone comes to the door). Everyone is resting up so they will eventually have the energy to take a nap.

A couple of years went by and Nigel slowly but surely warmed up to us. He would come sleep in my bed at night, though nowhere near me or any of the other dogs. But at least it was something. He was putting a little bit of effort in to being a part of the family. And sometimes he would follow me around the house, although three feet behind me; just out of arms reach. If I turned to look at him or spoke to him, he'd take off running and hide. But for him, he seemed happy enough. He had his gang and he had his routine, and that was all he needed. He was pretty low maintenance in the way that he didn't want your attention or affection, but pretty high maintenance when you had to listen to his barking all day long. And he had to go to the groomer. Well, for that to happen, you had to catch him. Which wasn't easy. When I would call the groomer I would get the latest appointment possible so I could spend the day catching him. Again, he was a very street smart and savvy dog. If I couldn't quickly corner him and he could get me in a situation where I had to chase him around a large object, like a sofa, I knew I was in for a long morning and a lot of exercise.

One day we had to do an emergency butt shaving on Nigel. This is a common occurrence when you have a long haired dog.

Too much fur and too much poop make for an unpleasant and uncomfortable situation. We caught him relatively quickly because he was in such distress from his butt situation he couldn't run as fast as normal. Erik got out the electric clippers and while we were doing the nasty chore, Nigel squirmed out of Erik's grasp and fell to the floor. Nigel took off and it was another few hours before we could get close to him. It was then that I noticed Nigel was limping. He had torn his toenail pretty badly. It was bleeding all over the place and hanging there by the quick, which you know has got to hurt. Just saying the word "quick" as it relates to a toenail makes me feel queasy.

A few days went by and it wasn't getting better, it was getting worse. He had gotten to the point where he wouldn't walk on it at all. He wasn't eating. He was just shaking. And worst of all? He wasn't barking. So we decided he better make a trip to the vet. Luckily Nigel couldn't really run so catching him wasn't too bad. The car ride just about killed the poor guy. If it was possible to shake yourself to death he was going to do it. I couldn't really blame him though, if he had indeed been one of the puppy mill Maltese that were in the car accident, his last ride hadn't been too great of an experience for him. We got him all checked in and the vet came over and quickly looked at the nail and said it would have to be removed. The vet touched Nigel's nail with his pinkie finger and the nail fell off. Really. Just like that. We were all a little surprised. But not Nigel. He didn't even notice. The vet shrugged his shoulders and wrapped Nigel's foot up in a bandage, which Nigel promptly removed in less than twelve seconds after we got back in the car. We went on our merry way…two hundred and twenty dollars lighter in the bank account. We've since learned to be more cautious when handling Nigel. And we've also learned to be a little more proactive and less reactive in our diagnosis of non-life threatening ailments before we go to the vet.

Nigel blended in very well with the other dogs, but several years after the toenail incident, something quite strange and unexpected happened. Nigel fell in love. And he fell in love with the most unexpected of all the dogs here. Her name is Edith. Now, this sort of thing sometimes happens at the Sanctuary, but when it does, it is presented to us in a way that lets us know that Cupid has a very strange sense of humor. The love pairings are definitely odd, if not downright freakish.

There is Rosie and Stanley. Rosie is a terminally ill rat terrier. She is only about ten (which is young for this place), tall, beautiful and bossy. Her boyfriend is Stanley. Stanley is a tiny, five pound, sixteen year old, very crabby Chihuahua. He is blind and deaf, but he knows when Rosie is near. It was love at first sight for Rosie…probably not Stanley since he is blind, but they still fell in love immediately. Which is strange because Stanley hates all the other dogs. And Rosie, being a Rat Terrier stalks the other Chihuahuas that live here and terrorizes them relentlessly. She gets this intense look on her face and follows poor Chester around like he is going to be her next meal. She chases Wilkie, another small Chihuahua, at every available opportunity. So Wilkie spends most of his time in the relative safety of the back room areas. Yet, besides all of this, Rosie is always kind and loving to Stanley. When she lays on the couch, he stands on top of her and licks her for hours on end and she loves it. If she sees me carrying Stanley, she starts to whimper and jump in excitement. She won't let anyone pick on him. She lets him do whatever he wants to her, where she barely tolerates the other dogs and has been known to take several of them down a couple of pegs for no reason. If another dog even gets within five feet of Stanley when he is eating, he attacks. But Stanley saves his food for Rosie and lets her eat out of his bowl.

Other odd couples of note would include Norman and, well, everyone. Poor Norman gets humped almost constantly. I'm not sure what pheromones he's putting off, but everyone loves it, males and females alike. Chester, the super-tiny Chihuahua and the extra-large dachshund, Maxine, are extremely fond of each other. And Zelda, the true loner of the Sanctuary, could never get enough of a blind, deaf and mute dachshund from Nebraska who went by the name of Henry. She even let Henry move into her closet which she usually spends all day guarding so no one can set foot inside.

But as unpredictable as all those relationships were, Nigel and Edith take the proverbial cake. Edith, or "Little Edie," as she is known, is a round, short, sort of Brussels Griffon terrier mix...thing. She is blind from a severe head injury, has a terrible under bite, and suffers from some sort of doggie schizophrenia. The day we brought Little Edie home from the shelter, we made a pit stop at my mother-in-law's house (well, actually just her lawn) to see if Little Edie had to go potty. Little Edie was still groggy from a surgery that she had that morning, so she slowly wandered around the yard and was extremely mellow. We got her home and she promptly went to sleep. The next morning, it was as though her soul was taken over by another dog. Little Edie, literally, walked across the kitchen floor on her hind legs. Backwards. Barking and wagging her tail the entire time. And she is able to match her high level of unbridled joy with unbridled anger. She can immediately devolve into a bossy, fearless, angry and mean fighter. She is either a lover or a fighter. There is no middle ground with her.

Little Edie came to us without a name. We named her after a character in the documentary film Grey Gardens. It is a movie chronicling the daily lives of the aunt (Big Edie) and first cousin (Little Edie) of former U.S. First Lady Jacqueline Kennedy Onassis. The mother and daughter duo lived together for five decades in a dilapidated mansion in East Hampton with limited funds while descending in to ever-increasing squalor and isolation. It is an entertaining documentary, and Little Edie Bouvier Beale is a fascinating character. Interestingly, Little Edie Bouvier Beale had a bizarre medical issue that caused her hair to fall out and never grow back. And, in a case of life imitating art imitating life imitating art documenting life, our Little Edie has the same problem. A few years ago, Little Edie's fur was covered with mats and so Erik shaved her, but the hair just never grew back. Little Edie Bouvier Beale had a vanity issue with being bald, so she always wore a head-wrap and a hat. Our Little Edie could not care any less that she was bald. She is just happy to be fed twice a day. And if she gets to fight somebody every now and then, well, that is just a bonus!

Humble Nigel is the exact opposite of Little Edie. He is tiny, timid and shy. And he has no shortage of hair. But he loves Edith. His love for her didn't blossom right away like it did with Rosie and Stanley. We had Edie for a few years before we noticed his crush. Perhaps he had actually loved her all along and it just took him a few years to get up the courage to let her know. Now, Little Edie doesn't like anyone near her. But no matter how much growling and snapping she does, Nigel will brave the storm and curl up with her nonetheless. When she finally falls asleep, he will start grooming her. He will lick her eyes, make sure her ears are clean, and then licks her front teeth which stick out of her mouth due to the under bite. She would never tolerate this sort of forward behavior if she were awake, and Nigel is risking his very life every time he does this, but he loves her so much and knows he can only get away with kissing her while she is sleeping. He also tries to mate with her. A lot. He will start out slowly and carefully, much the male black widow would, lest the female accidently wake up and feel obligated to eat his head. He follows her everywhere. He lets her eat his dinner. He saves his treats for her. He used to sleep in my bed with me, but that has all changed and he will only sleep wherever Little Edie is. Nigel is sort of scared to go outside, but Edith loves being outside. So when she goes out, Nigel will lie in a certain spot in front of the gate in the hallway. He will stay there as long as Edith is outside...keeping watch. As soon as I open the back door, Nigel gets up and runs to the door and waits for Little Edie to come back in. Nigel is very afraid of thunder and before Little Edie was around, he would find me or a pile of laundry to huddle with. But with Little Edie in his life, when it thunders, he will go right to her for comfort. The piles of laundry and, yes, even me, have become obsolete. Now that's love.

Understand that Edith will be growling and fussing through all of this, but she'll never leave. She'll never just get up and walk away, though she has every opportunity to do just that. I think she secretly loves it. I think she was initially surprised by Nigel's love, but the surprised turned into flattery. And then she came to just expect his love. I mean, Edith is one messed up cookie. She has a crazy, drug-addicted, homeless look about her. Nigel is an expensive, highly coveted purebred purse dog. Not the kind of guy Edith usually attracts, I'm sure. But true love knows no boundaries.

So their life is good. As of this writing, we've had Nigel about six years, and Little Edie for almost four. He's still madly in love and planning on proposing to Little Edie as soon as he can save up enough money for the wedding.

As for the new white dog that Oliver forewarned us about? Well about a month after finding Nigel, and then finding out he wasn't the prophesized little white dog, I got a call from the shelter. They had a dog that had been thrown out the window of a moving car, in a box, that was going thirty five miles an hour. She had suffered a pretty severe head injury and had also injured her back hips and couldn't currently walk. My heart stopped. Trying to sound casual and almost disinterested, I asked, "What does she look like?" The volunteer said, "Well, she is little, old and white." Of course...of course she is. Oliver recognized her the moment we brought her home. He pointed at her and said, "See, it's the white dog. Her name is Baby Rose." And then Oliver went back to watching Finding Nemo, again, and life was back to normal.

Three Blind Mice...Wait. What?!

It was a typical evening at the Sanctuary, my husband and I were cleaning. I walked in the bedroom to ask my husband if we had any more paper towels and found him standing there with one of those metal "catch it alive and then drive it twenty miles out to the middle of nowhere and let it go and pretend it has a chance to live" mouse traps. I didn't know that we even had those any more, after my son was traumatized a few years earlier by a release that we did at a park five miles away from our house. Oliver was confused that we were releasing mice, who had a home...ours, into a field, where there was no home for them to live in. Erik pointed out that there were lots of holes for them to live in, but Oliver pointed out that the holes were not heated with a wood-burning stove and didn't contain any food like cereal and dry dog food. Erik had nothing for this, and we were forced to buy Oliver a Thomas the Train character to get him to stop crying and Erik swore off the live traps.

And yet, here we were, with my husband holding one in his hands and peering inside. I asked him what was going on and he sort of stammered that it looked like a mouse had her babies in the closet but then got stuck in the trap and couldn't get out, because, well, it's a trap. Then I heard it. For the very first time I heard the tiny squeals that were to become the bane of our existence for the next two months. I still hear them now, but in my nightmares. And then, there it was. There was a tiny baby on the floor right in front of me. I'd almost stepped on it. It looked like a lima bean with a tail. No hair, just a squealing mass of tail and mouth. I was instantly in love.

Erik and I heard more squeaking and took the few geriatric dogs that were in the room and put them in the hallway. Thank God they were deaf. I looked around and found two more babies behind the dresser. I had Erik search the closet, two more. We searched and searched until we were sure that we had all of them. They must have been so hungry that they were squirming around looking for their mom. I asked Erik if the mom was alive, he said yes. I asked him what he was going to do, he said he would figure something out and took the trap with mom inside and the babies down to the garage.

Now, I have to tell you my husband is a horrible liar. I mean, certainly there are worse traits to have, but I could tell by his nervous demeanor and the fact that his head was starting to sweat a bit (always a dead giveaway) that I wasn't getting the full story. Turns out he had put the trap in the closet and didn't check it for a few days until he heard the babies squealing for their mom.

I went down to the garage and found Erik sitting there looking extremely dumbfounded and a bit sheepish. I asked him again if the mom was alive, he paused, I could see his brain scrambling to come up with something to tell me and his eyes were shifting back and forth and he started sweating…then he said, "no." So here we were with eight babies and a dead mom. Now, I ask you, the reader, in all honesty, what would you have done? Because over the course of the next two months I asked myself that question repeatedly. What would a normal person have done in this situation? They say that hindsight is always 20/20. But, on the topic of the baby mice, my hindsight is really, really blurry. I don't know if I would have done what I was about to do, but I also don't know what else I could have done. It was certainly a tricky situation.

I immediately ran upstairs and started searching on Google what to do with newborn mice. The advice was much the same...you can try to save them, but it isn't going to work. There is no hope. These mice will not survive. But if you are crazy enough to try, get yourself some kitten or puppy formula, a syringe, a heating pad, some blankets and a box. Wow. Really? You mean stuff I have here, right now, at the house? Life is never this easy. Was this a sign that what I was about to embark upon was what was supposed to happen, and the choice I was making was the right choice?

I gathered up my supplies, made a comfy box with a heating pad and blankets and got to work. At this point there were eight babies. It was now time to try and feed them. I have a mom's sixth sense about formula temperature, and the magic numbers this time were three tablespoons of liquid formula in the microwave on high for nine seconds. Perfect. Now, over the years, I have accumulated a fairly impressive syringe collection, but I didn't have a syringe small enough for their tiny mouths. I mean their entire body was an inch long at the most. And that was when they were stretching. So I decided to use the tip of a child's watercolor paint brush dipped in formula to try to feed them. But I also had to do this without getting it in their nose which is, to use a technical medical term, about a hairline from their mouth. If they had gotten any in their little noses, then it would have gotten in their little lungs, and then, all of a sudden, they are in huge trouble. I could see this was going to take practice.

Almost immediately we had two die. They were the two that hadn't been very responsive when we had found them on the floor of the bedroom. But, I consoled myself. They died in a warm box covered with a handmade heirloom baby blanket with a crazy woman desperately trying to save them. I hoped the effort counted for something. We took the two deceased mice and wrapped them in a lacy vintage handkerchief and put them in a Ziploc bag and popped them in our freezer, which doubles as the morgue at our house. I wedged them down in between the sweet little baby chick we had lost late last year, frozen pancakes, several pints of Haagen-

Dazs ice cream, my son's hermit crab and a box that I had clearly forgotten what the contents were…was that the guinea pig?

And then, just like every time we experience death here at the Sanctuary, there wasn't much time to grieve. It was very quickly time to give all our focus back to the survivors. After I convinced myself that everyone had at least one drop of formula in their bellies, I put them on the heating pad, covered them up with their blanket and put them in the bathroom (which was to become the mouse nursery) and turned off the light. After doing more research on the internet I found out that you have to feed the babies every two hours for six weeks. EVERY TWO HOURS FOR SIX WEEKS. Not every two hours during the day, but every two hours, day and night. Oh dear.

Now, let me tell you a little something about my husband. He loves to sleep. He craves it like a drug. Before we were married, he would work fourteen hours a day and then come home and sleep for nine hours and wake up and go back to work and he would spend his entire day off sleeping and he was fine with that. Totally fine. He was convinced that if he got less than nine hours of sleep a day, he would die. And not only does he love sleep, he's really good at it. I knew he was the perfect man for me when I realized he could sleep through the cacophony of dozens of dogs barking, one of them a tiny Chihuahua standing on his head, my son screaming from an ear infection all night, his alarm going off repeatedly not a foot from his head, a dog puking on his back, nothing woke this man up. Would the guilt of killing a mama who had eight babies to care for be enough to rouse him…every two hours? My husband has a heart of gold, so I was betting yes.

So, I promptly set my iPhone alarm to go off every two hours. I had the day shift. From the 5:30 a.m. feeding until the 9:30 p.m. feeding, I was on duty. Mostly, because Erik was at work. Then Erik started at 11:30 p.m. and ended with the 3:30 a.m. feeding. We lost two more babies over the next few days. Four left. Now, not only did we have to mix a fresh batch of perfectly warm formula every time we went to feed them, but after feeding (which was the messiest thing you can imagine) we had to wash off their milk covered bodies with a q-tip dipped in warm water, otherwise they would become this horrible sticky milk mess. Their skin was as thin as rice paper, so being careful and gentle was of the utmost importance. One by one we would feed them, dipping the brush into the formula time and time and time again until the babies were full. We had to hurry, or else the formula would get cold and then we would have to go re-heat it. Then we would give them a tiny q-tip bath, dry them off, kiss their little ears, nose and tail and pop them back into bed. Well, I would kiss them. I'm not sure that Erik did. The entire feeding process took about forty five minutes each time, from making the formula to tucking in the last little body. There was barely enough time to go back to sleep before it was time to get up and start the process all over again.

After two weeks, my husband was starting to look a bit dazed from sleep deprivation. I was constantly feeling like I was forgetting something...did I feed them? Did I feed Oliver? Did I feed me? What time is it? What is my name?

We lost one more but again, he died warm and full. The remaining three were doing well. They were very hungry and started squirming around so much I had to get a taller box so they wouldn't climb out. They hadn't opened their eyes yet, but they were starting to grow a tiny bit of fur which was covered in dried formula. I have to admit, I was deeply in love with them. I loved the way they would hold the tiny paint brush in their hands while they sucked from it. I loved how they would squirm with their mouths open as wide as they could waiting for the warm milk. I loved how they looked all bunched up sleeping. Like wrinkled, old, naked homeless men.

This all happened in October and suddenly we were presented with a problem. This was the time of year that we always take Oliver to the Anderson Farm's Pumpkin Patch Fall Festival. A family tradition. And we don't really have many family traditions, so it was important for us that we go. The Pumpkin Patch Fall Festival is an all-day event about an hour and a half away from our home, but it is worth the drive. Apart from the pumpkin cannon, gourd slingshot, mine car ride, forty acre corn maze, farm animals (including buffalo,) gem and fossil mining, and the wildly unhealthy (yet tasty) food, it is one of the few things we actually do as a family. It certainly fits the "something for everybody" moniker and little Oliver looks forward to it the most.

But how were we going to manage this? I didn't want to disappoint my son. I could see him in therapy in the future saying that his mom loved the mice more than she loved him. I considered hiring a mouse-sitter to come up and feed those babies every two hours, but could not think of anyone even remotely qualified. So we did what any normal people would do in this situation, we brought them with us. I had some of those air-activated hand warmer packs that Erik and Oliver use when they go sledding in sub-zero weather, a cooler for the formula, an ice pack in case they got too warm and an outdoor thermometer to tell us if we needed more "hot" or more "cold."

We drove them to the pumpkin patch, left them in the car (with the windows cracked) and every two hours, either Erik or I would run out and feed them. Erik didn't have any problems, he is older, bald, has a full beard, doesn't smile much and is the kind of guy that people don't get caught staring at. On the other hand, when I was sitting in the passenger seat of my car with baby mice in my lap, feeding one with a paintbrush, some people pulled into the space next to me and I could see a man peering in looking confused (and mildly disturbed) as to what I was doing. I felt embarrassed, exposed, like I was sitting in the car smoking crack. But, again, the question that keeps appearing throughout this story remains front and center…what else could I have done?

So, the three blind mice were doing well. Two of them started opening their eyes, which was difficult because they were typically sealed shut from dried formula. The baths weren't doing their jobs, and they didn't have a mom to lick the milk off. I know you probably don't believe it, but I do have some boundaries. We were well into month two and could now go maybe three and a half hours in between feedings. It felt like a vacation. I had so much free time! Erik was looking less sleep deprived. I could remember what day it was. It was pure bliss!

And then, with no warning and much to our dismay, we lost another. I had been concerned because he was the one who didn't move around much and didn't really want to eat more than a few drops. Into the freezer he went with his siblings. He died warm, full, and having been to the pumpkin patch.

Only two left, and one was a dynamo. A total firecracker. That mouse tried to escape the box any way he could. With his tiny toenails, he would climb the cord to the heating pad and he would scale blankets. I had to put them in a large Tupperware that was slippery so he couldn't climb out. The other, more docile baby, just wanted to be handfed and sleep (much like my husband). Another few weeks went by and we lost one more. We didn't lose the dynamo. No. We lost the one that exhibited the same traits as my husband, the sleeper. This didn't go unnoticed by my husband, who made an effort to sleep less and interact more. So something good came of it. But the bottom line, at this point, was that we only had one mouse left. Which was still pretty good, considering we were supposed to have none two days after all this mess started.

Our single, remaining mouse had opened his eyes and had fur. The fur was matted up with formula. I tried bathing him, but dried formula is quite a bit like concrete. One day I was tugging on his fur a bit to get a glob of formula off and his entire fur coat came off in my hand. Not just a chunk or a patch...all of it. Like he had been wearing a tiny, fur mouse suit. I totally freaked out. I mean, I don't know what I was expecting when I cleaned him, but I certainly wasn't expecting this. His skin was bright red and his eyes bulged out from his newly bare face. I thought he would die for sure, but he actually seemed happier and somehow liberated with his crusty confining mouse suit gone. Now his q-tip bath was a breeze, no yucky dried formula. And, very quickly, all of his fur grew back. As my husband is fond of saying, "No harm, no foul."

So eventually our little mouse could drink the formula on his own. I would pour it into a little, plastic milk jug lid for him. I started putting in little bits of food for him to eat. Once I was convinced he could eat I transferred him to nicely prepared mouse cage. It had an exercise wheel, lots of bedding to hide in, his blankie, a water bottle (I wasn't convinced he could use) some toys and lots of food. I still put a capful of formula in each day just in case he couldn't figure out the water bottle. His new home was in my craft room. I still had the heating pad under his cage because you know, I'm his mom, I want him to be so warm he's sweating and so full he feels sick.

One morning I went in and he was not in his cage. The lid was partially open and he was gone. I did notice mouse droppings on my sewing machine and around the room, so I figured he was just expanding his territory a bit. Now, again, I don't know what a normal person would have done at this point, but after what we'd been through, what could I do? I left the lid open on his cage, put a scarf in the cage and down the side to the floor so he could climb back in if he needed to, and continued to fill his food bowl with his favorite Lucky Charms. Each morning I would go in and see the food container empty. I would find Lucky Charms in the strangest places.

Then I noticed his food dish was remaining full. I had come to the conclusion he had moved out. I felt betrayed. Not betrayed enough to remove the cage just in case he needed to move back home for a while, but it did sting a bit. I then began to wonder what it would feel like when my own son moves out and goes off to college. I started to feel panicky. Unsettled. Out of sorts. And then profoundly sad. But then I remembered that I am a grown woman living in the United States of America and I can do whatever the hell I want. So I will just follow Oliver. Simple as that. And I immediately felt better. But I was still worried about the mouse.

Well, about a month went by with no letters, no phone calls, not even a text. Then one day I opened my coat closet and he popped out of a hole he had chewed in the pocket of my expensive wool coat and just sat there and looked at me. I knew it was my mouse because he didn't run. He wouldn't let me grab him, he would stay just out of my reach, but he just sat there staring. So, I shut the door and smiled. I know, I know, you shouldn't just have mice living in your house, eating your best wool coat, stashing dog food in every drawer, boot, purse and skein of yarn you own, but this was my mouse. What could I do? I was just hoping that HE would not meet a SHE who would again bless us with a family to feed EVERY TWO HOURS after my husband accidently kills her.

A few more months went by. I felt happy thinking about my mouse living large. I would see holes in the dog food bags and get a warm feeling in my heart. Then one morning, it was all to come to an end. I noticed something floating in the dog's water bowl. I got closer and noticed it was a mouse. I tried to pull it out and resuscitate it, but it wasn't to be. He was gone. I was in a state of shock. I didn't know if it was my mouse, I kept telling myself it couldn't be. I was horrified I had killed any mouse. I threw out all the big, glass dog bowls and replaced them with shallow, abrasive bowls that a mouse could climb out of. I was heartbroken. I walked around for days feeling like I had murdered that mouse. Well, maybe more like man-slaughter; it wasn't premeditated. Certainly much more of an accident than my husband with the so-called "live" trap. I never had any intention of killing him. Obviously.

But was it really him? I slipped into the river of denial, but after a few weeks, I had to face the facts. I didn't see my mouse around anymore, so it must be true. After all I had done, after all that we'd been through, yes, I was finally forced to come to terms with the fact that it was my mouse that had drown in the dog's bowl. I was absolutely devastated and the grieving process began. I had not been this sad in a long time.

And then, like with everything in my life at one point or another, I got some honest perspective on the matter. Perspective I was actually willing to listen to. I was telling my friend Lori about the mouse (she had been there since the birth). Lori looked at me, took my hand, and calmly told me that I had obviously failed him as a mother...I hadn't taught him how to swim.

Duke Elway

Duke was an impossibly old beagle who belonged to my husband's friend. My husband's friend loved Duke, but loved his wife more. His wife thought it was "time" for Duke, he was older, deaf and she was afraid he'd bite their new grandbaby. So instead of letting them euthanize Duke, we brought him here to live.

For Erik, it was like having an old friend move in with us, but I wasn't so sure about Duke. I'd never had a beagle before, and he'd lived with the same family for his entire life. My husband remembered when his friend got Duke, just a tiny puppy at eight weeks old from a mall pet store. His full name is Duke Elway. Erik's friend (and Erik) are really big Denver Broncos fans.

While waiting for Duke to move in, I worried that since he was so old and had only had one home for his whole life, he would lay around all day being depressed, thinking of his family. I was afraid that he would miss his old life. I was afraid that he would be miserable. I was afraid his spirit would be broken and he would constantly bay in that stereotypical beagle way, just waiting for sweet death to come and whisk him away. And it turns out that I couldn't have been more wrong. Well, about everything except the horrible, constant beagle-bay thing, which, it turns out, they also do when they are happy. And Duke was a happy boy, that's for sure. A happy, happy boy. And he let us know it. Everyday.

Duke walked through our front door and never looked back. I don't even remember him saying goodbye to his previous owner. It was as if he'd lived with us forever, as if we had purchased him from the horrible pet store when he was just a baby, but then he went to go live with my husband's friend for sixteen years, all the while knowing that he would end up with us, his real family. And Erik knew Duke really well. He was the four-legged companion on many a fishing and hiking trip. Erik knew Duke when Duke would run a mile ahead on the hiking trail and be loud and energetic and crazy and bark at rattlesnakes and wreak havoc. So there was already a history with Duke. A good, fun history.

But don't get me wrong, it wasn't that Duke loved us and showered us with affection for saving him from the ultimate sleep. It was just as if this was his house and he allowed us to live here with him so he could bite our hands, steal our food and drive us insane with that beagle bark of his. He took ownership of us.

So in Duke's previous home, he had rules. You know, the standard dog rules. No begging at the table, no getting up on the furniture, no biting the hand that feeds you, regular kind of stuff. We, on the other hand, have very few rules. One rule is you can't bite Oliver. The second rule is…oh, there isn't a second rule. We keep things pretty simple around here. There is enough complication in our lives just from diagnosing health issues and figuring out who spewed the mystery fluid on the kitchen floor. So we just stick to one rule at the house. But it is strictly enforced. Biting Oliver will most likely get you ejected from the Sanctuary (unless you are a tiny Chihuahua like Chico and easily removed from a potential biting situation), but if you are fortunate enough to gain Oliver's favor (which only a few dogs have) you are golden. Oliver is the Emperor. A thumbs up or a thumbs down is huge. But, Oliver's thumbs are usually set squarely in the middle. He is an ambivalent ruler.

Now I know Duke's previous mistress was afraid he would bite the grandbaby. I wasn't sure why she thought this, but I figured she probably had her reasons. At this time Oliver was only about three years old. Should I have been concerned for Oliver? Yes. But I wasn't. Should I have been concerned for Erik and myself? No. Should I have been? Absolutely.

With each day that went by Duke got younger. This is a strange phenomenon that we witness time and time again here at the Sanctuary. We have scores of Benjamin Button's running around the place. Dogs that can barely walk over the threshold are running circles around the yard at full speed in a matter of weeks. Duke was no exception. We think it has something to do with the altitude. He walked through that door stiff and slow with his head down. Now he was jumping on the couch, prancing through the house, barking and baying at great length. We've had dogs that we were told wouldn't live a month and three years later, there they are, begging for dinner. Loudly. With a lot of over-animated facial contortions and jumping.

Duke had two loves in his life. One was sleeping on the furniture. He had been denied this luxury in his previous life, so he was taking full advantage of it now. He'd spend his day going to each piece of furniture in the house, taking a nap, and then moving on to the next piece of furniture. I heard a rumor that in his old situation he would sleep in the laundry room on a doormat. Now he was in the middle of the king-sized bed on the electric blanket, thumbing through the premium satellite TV channels and sipping his second Strawberry daiquiri. All before breakfast. Yeah, it was all good.

The other love of his life was eating. But particularly eating things he wasn't allowed to eat. He loved to steal Oliver's food from him. He'd grab a vegetarian chicken nugget right out of Oliver's hand. His favorite thing was a "Cosmic Brownie." This is a strange chemical-tasting brick in the shape of a brownie covered with "sprinkles" that look like lawn fertilizer. They are four hundred empty calories of pseudo-food and chemicals. It was, and still is, Oliver's prime choice of dessert. Oliver only has two or three bites of it, so we don't feel too badly about him eating it.

Duke would spend his day lying on his chair of choice scheming on how to get that evening's Cosmic Brownie. This would, of course, send Oliver into fits of tears. But no matter how much Duke wanted that sorry excuse for food, he was never aggressive towards Oliver. We were always worried that Duke would get ill after eating the stolen brownie, but we came to the conclusion that there probably wasn't a trace of chocolate in the "chocolate" Cosmic Brownie, so no worries there. I think that they were allowed to call it "chocolate" because it has a chocolate color to it. The worst that we figured could happen is that the brownie would embalm Duke from the inside out and turn him into some sort of zombie dog. But, like a lot of dogs here, he was probably already halfway there.

Now, while Duke never showed any aggression towards Oliver, he was certainly saving it up for me and Erik. He had no qualms about biting us if he didn't want to do something. If I tried to move him over so I could sit on the couch too, he'd nearly rip my arm off. If I tried to discipline him during the brownie heist, he'd bite my hands. It was strange because Duke wasn't a mean dog. I think that since there was food involved, he was just defending himself in a very primal, physical way. He was always ready for a fight. Survival of the fittest. And Duke was a born survivor.

But despite his nasty disposition at times and the wounds rapidly covering Erik's arms, we loved Duke. We really did. He was so happy. He loved it here so much. We had heard tales about beagles getting lost from following their noses. Typical story. The dog gets out the front door or the back gate. He catches the scent of a fox or a raccoon or a squirrel or a deer and he's off. Walking and sniffing, sniffing and walking. Never looking up. Just following his nose. Sniffing and walking and walking and sniffing out in to the middle of the forest, finally lifting his head hours later and having no idea where he is. Miles and miles away from home. And then they are lost. Forever. Since we live only half a mile from Pike National Forest, this was a big fear of ours, and caused my husband a lot of anxiety. I mean, Duke belonged to Erik's friend. And, even though his friend was extremely grateful for Erik and me to take care of Duke, I know that Erik felt an extra obligation to Duke. He had known him for decades.

But, out of all the dogs we've ever had, the one to not worry about running away was Duke. We could let him out the front door and he'd go potty and come right back in. He never once tried to get away. There were no comfy chairs, blankets or Cosmic Brownies out there in the big, bad world…he just wanted back inside the house. And I don't blame him.

One time we all left the house for several hours. When we came back and pulled into our driveway we noticed Duke standing on the porch. I initially thought we had forgotten to let Duke back in before we left, then I noticed the front door was open. Wide open. Erik and I panicked. I mean, we had over a dozen dogs who had access to the front door when we left, how many of them were going to be missing? We jumped out of the car and ran up to the porch. Quick head count. How many are missing? Two? Five? Nine? How about none.

Most of them were actually still in the house sitting close to the front door, even though the door was wide open. A few were sunning themselves on the porch. Duke was standing at the top of the stairs, tail wagging, waiting for us to come home. The blind ones couldn't wander off because Duke was blocking the way. Duke knew what Nirvana is, not only for himself but for all the others. And he knew that it was here. And not outside. It was inside. On the soft pillows.

Even when we'd give him a bone, Duke wouldn't go outside with it. He decided the carpet was just as good as dirt and would spend hours "burying" a bone in the carpet with his nose. Which always led to two things. A bone that he'd spent hours burying would by lying out in full view on the carpet, and a bloody nose for Duke from rug burns. But he'd keep trying.

As the days went by and all of us were getting older, Duke was still getting younger and younger. He could do things that no senior dog should be able to do. I mean, one of the blessings of having a house full of seniors is that they mostly just sleep. No puppy mischief. No teenager antics. This is supposed to be a retirement home. Where your life is gearing down. But Duke had different ideas. His energy level just kept going up and up and up and up. He enjoyed going for walks, on leash, and then coming home and running around like a lunatic for half an hour. When Erik's friend would come to visit, he barely recognized Duke. Erik's friend is convinced we have the fountain of youth at our home. Erik and I wish we did, especially in the mornings when we have to clean the floors.

It was nearing Christmas time and Duke had been with us several months. I was still working at my job outside of the home and we were having a cookie exchange at work. I had picked this wonderful recipe for "triple death by chocolate cookies." These cookies were the real deal. Dark chocolate chips, loaded with cocoa powder, iced with chocolate frosting. I made about ten dozen of them, placed a dozen each in cookie tins and had put them in a large cardboard box. I put the box in the middle of the kitchen table, pulled out the chairs so nobody could get on the table and went to get dressed. I was brushing my teeth when I heard a commotion. I went upstairs to see what was going on and what to my wondering eyes should appear? Duke, standing in the middle of the kitchen table eating my triple death by chocolate cookies. He had managed to get on the table – how? I'll never know, tip the cardboard box, get the lid off the cookie tins and had eaten about two dozen cookies before he was caught. I was so upset that I thought this near imminent "death by chocolate" was exactly what he deserved. But then my anger subsided and I started to get very worried. These weren't cosmic chemical brownies, these were pure chocolate, the kind of chocolate you are warned time and time again will kill your dog. We called the vet and he told us to give Duke hydrogen peroxide to get him to expel the cookies. We gave him the first dose...nothing. We gave him a second dose, still nothing. I had to rush off to work, worried that this might be the last time I saw Duke. Erik stayed home to monitor him. Once at work with my eight dozen cookies, I called Erik every hour. No, Duke never threw up from the peroxide. And he never got sick. Nothing. No diarrhea, no vomiting. When I got home Duke was sleeping peacefully on the couch after eating his dinner. It was, and still is the biggest mystery as to why those cookies didn't kill him. Erik and I came to the conclusion that Duke was just too happy to die.

But, alas, Duke did die. His soul was young, but his heart was old. He never ran away. And he never bit Oliver. And we miss his annoying, beagle bark. But only sometimes.

All Creatures, Great and Gross

So you've probably figured out by now that I'm a huge animal lover. Not just dogs, but all kinds of animals. Over the years I've had just about every kind of pet (intentional or unintentional) that you can imagine. From a bunny to a bunch of Madagascar Hissing Cockroaches. Here are some of the more memorable stories about what we call, All Creatures, Great and Gross.

The Wasps

I used to live in Texas. Pflugerville to be exact. Where everything that should begin with the letter "F" begins with "Pf." Businesses. Roads. Children. As a native of Colorado, moving to Texas was a huge shock to my system. Even though Colorado gets over three hundred days of sunshine a year, apparently I had no idea what it was like to actually be hot. And humidity? I never could have imagined such torture. Wearing shorts and flip-flops outside on Christmas morning? Really? I also remember living in Colorado and complaining about the mosquitoes and moths. Little did I realize that in Texas they are large enough to carry your firstborn out the back door and fly them all the way to Peru. Now that I'm back in Colorado, I will never again complain about a "hot" summer day, or a mosquito that is, well, the size of an actual mosquito.

In Texas, besides the mosquitoes, moths, heat, humidity and lack of traditional holiday weather, one of the biggest things I was unprepared for were the wasps. I mean, they were everywhere. I would venture to guess that there was a nest in every tree. Wasps were just something you had to live with, like the snakes, fire ants and scorpions. The only difference being that I was prepared for the snakes, fire ants and scorpions. They make the news. There are no shortage of TV shows about them on the Discovery Channel. Even Africanized honey bees make the news in some horrific tragedy every few months. Wasps? Not so much.

Right after my son was born, some wasps decided to build a large nest right outside of my back door. Of course they weren't there before my son was born. No. They had to wait until I was getting an hour of sleep a day so I could stress out about them while being sleep deprived and nervous about being a new mom. And no matter how stealthy I was, every time I opened the door to get to the back yard, I would disturb them and a bunch of them would fly out to investigate.

I have a "live and let live" policy with most things and didn't have any personal issues with the wasps, but I was pretty worried having an infant around them. And the dog door was also right next to the back door and the large wasp's nest and I would not have been surprised if Peabody had a rare, highly sensitive and shockingly expensive wasp allergy. Not to a wasp sting, mind you. Peabody was such a medical anomaly that he would have been allergic to the sound of their wings.

So what to do? I know you can buy those cans of wasp spray that can shoot a stream of death like 12 feet, so you can douse the wasps and maybe even yourself with toxic poison from a relatively safe distance, but I couldn't imagine killing them. Wasps are complex and beautiful creatures. I mean, who doesn't envy that tiny waist? They hadn't done anything to me, and I didn't wish them harm. I just wanted them to relocate. The karma that might come back to bite me from murdering an entire hive of wasps was something I didn't want to be looking over my shoulder for. Never underestimate karma.

I decided to take the much less logical, but much kinder route, I was going to relocate them myself. Now I knew that bees couldn't fly if their wings got wet, and I assumed that it applied to wasps as well. I also knew they left their nest early in the morning. So the very next day I was up very early armed with a spray bottle of water, a long stick, some super glue, duct tape and several large pieces of cardboard.

Many of the wasps were already hovering around the nest. I would wait for them to land on something and then I would mist them with the spray bottle. You had to do it very lightly so you that you didn't drown them. When they were wet and unable to fly I would scoop them up on the pieces of cardboard. Then I would tap the nest with my long stick and more wasps would come out. I repeated this process until I was pretty sure the nest was somewhat empty. Then I misted the wasps one more time for good measure and got on a ladder and pulled the nest down by its stem. I relocated it to a tree in the front yard on a low branch. I glued the stem of the nest to the branch and then taped it with duct tape to make sure it stayed. I ran the pieces of cardboard with the wasps over to the newly located nest and propped them against the tree. When the wasps started drying they started flying. Some flew right into the nest (yes!) some flew back to where the nest used to be and hovered around looking confused. Others stayed glued to the cardboard. I decided to go inside and let nature take its course.

When I came back outside several hours later, the wasps seemed to have reinhabited their hive. A few were flying aimlessly around the back door but for the most part the move was a success. We had only a few casualties that had become stuck to the cardboard. I buried these in the dirt below the hive and said a few words.

I want to mention that I have never been stung by a bee or a wasp. I've heard that bees and wasps have a highly complex communication system. I think word got around and I'm on the "do not sting" list.

Rats!

Okay, so another new found joy of living in Texas was the rats. In Colorado if you saw a rat the size of a domestic cat in your house you would freak out and probably call 911. Rats aren't something you have in Colorado. You have tiny, cute little mice and small rats that can almost pass as rats, but a real, honest to god stereotypical "sewer rat" rat? That was the stuff of television. And movies. Horror movies. And living in the sewers underneath New York. Or so I thought. But after moving to Texas I realized that among other nasty things, you also get rats. Big, mean rats.

The first sign of the rats was a sound emanating from the attic. Initially I thought it was just mice, but it would have had to have been one big mouse to be making that kind of noise. So I put a live mouse trap in the attic. Nothing. I still kept hearing the noise. Then I thought maybe it was a raccoon or possum. So I put a larger live trap up there. The next day there was a huge rat in the trap. When the rat saw me, he hit the side of the cage so hard he tipped it over. When I reached for the handle to bring the trap out of the attic he stuck his arms out and tried to scratch me. His razor sharp teeth were wrapped around the wire of the cage as he bloodied his mouth trying to chew through it. The whole situation was really frightening.

So I took the cage, threw a moving blanket over it and drove it down to a field about five miles or so from my house and let him go. Then I put the cage back up in the attic. This same scenario went on for days, and then weeks, until I had trapped about twelve rats. After catching the thirteenth rat, I got suspicious. All thirteen rats were the same size and same color. In fact, the only thing that wasn't the same was that each rat I caught was calmer and tamer than the previous one. Rat thirteen I took out of the cage and it slept in my lap on the five mile trip to the drop-off area. No, not really. But I think you get the point.

In reality, rat fourteen was so calm I could hand feed him through the wires of the cage. So while he was grasping the bars of his cage, reaching for the frosted flakes, I quickly painted two of his nails. It was just a hunch, but I felt we were old friends. Could I have been catching the same rat over and over? Well, I caught rat fifteen and guess what? He had a beautiful pink manicure. I had been feeding this rat so much "bait" he had gotten pretty fat. Next time I caught him I drove him for forty five minutes before dropping him off. I figured with his weight issue, he'd never make it back.

Well, the trap remained empty for over a month, so I figured "problem solved." The strange thing, though, was that the bait from the trap was always missing. I just figured it was probably mice who were too light to trip the trap. After having rats, mice didn't even seem worth the trouble of catching, so I didn't bother.

Then one day I was up in the attic getting out the boxes of Christmas decorations. This is always my favorite time of year. I love opening up the boxes and finding treasures I had forgotten about, and all the beautiful ornaments I've collected over the years. But this time the treasure I found was entirely different than what I was expecting. I opened one of the boxes and found a litter of baby rats. There were ten of them, newly born, eyes closed, no fur. I was sort of in shock. Then I saw something even more shocking. The peanut butter encrusted Cheetos I had been baiting the live trap with. The male rat I had been catching over and over that I thought was getting fat from me over-feeding him, was actually a female. A pregnant female. And that is why she needed those peanut butter Cheetos so much. You know how brutal those strange cravings can be when you're pregnant. So I did what any reasonable person would have done. I quickly closed the box back up and put it in the attic in the exact same spot I found it and hoped that by next Christmas they would have grown up and moved out. And, thankfully, they did.

The Guinea Pigs

So it was Christmas time and Erik and I were dating. It was going to be our first Christmas together as a couple. Now there is only one thing I ever want for Christmas. A living animal. That is all I ever ask for and I've never gotten it. But Erik was smitten with me and I was going to put him to the test. I decided it would be really fun to have guinea pigs, so that is what I put on my Christmas list. Keep in mind, I was thirty eight years old at this point and I had been putting a live animal on my Christmas list ever since I was old enough to write. And I had never gotten one. Ever. So I didn't actually think I was going to get it this year. Just let me say here, be careful what you wish for.

So we spent Christmas morning at my soon to be mother-in-law's house. It was one of those Christmas' you only dream of. There were gifts everywhere (my mother-in-law is very generous) and her house was beautifully decorated. My son was only two at the time, so he was just in awe. Erik and I were (and still are, by the way) madly in love. I thought it couldn't have been more perfect. That is until we were almost done opening gifts and then Erik handed me one last gift. I opened it and it was a book about guinea pigs. Then he came down the stairs carrying a cage that contained two glorious furry guinea pigs. Not a gift card to go buy them at a later date, but the real deal. I remember jumping into his arms and calling him the "best boyfriend ever." Which he was.

We finished off the day by oohing and aahing over my beautiful creatures. One was a calico with long hair. He would make these beautiful singing, talking, cooing noises. He was very friendly, loved being held and was sweet, gentle and tame. The other was a shy little white and red spotted thing. She was skittish and didn't really relish being held. She would run and hide in a cardboard paper towel roll when I reached in the cage. Later that evening when I was back home and Erik had left, I noticed that the calico guinea pig was acting funny. Sort of running in these short bursts and breathing heavily. I called Erik in a panic. I had no experience with guinea pigs and though I scoured my "how to" book, it didn't say anything about this. Erik seemed perplexed as to what we should do. So he did what any "best boyfriend ever" would do. He drove from his house to my house at midnight on Christmas Day, got the guinea pig and drove it to the emergency vet. That's an hour and a half of driving late on Christmas Day. He called me when he got there, but it had been too late. The guinea pig had died in route to the hospital. Or that is what he told me anyway. He may have just been parked around the corner with a dead guinea pig, trying to figure out how to break the news to me. But there is no good way to give somebody news like that. It was a sad, somber end to the best Christmas gift ever and to the poor guinea pig's life. But, as a silver lining, he officially died after midnight, so he didn't ruin Christmas forever. Which was considerate.

I was now left with one lonely and shy guinea pig. The logical plan would have been to re-home her, or just let her live out her life until she died. So what did I do? I got her a friend. Again...bad idea. Nonetheless, Erik went and picked me out a beautiful apricot guinea pig we named Eleanor. About a week after getting Eleanor, the remaining guinea pig died. Or Eleanor killed her. I wasn't home when it happened, and all I saw was a corpse, so there were no witnesses.

Eleanor was mean. She hated me. She stayed in her little guinea pig hut twenty four hours a day unless she decided to venture out to try to bite me as I put food in her bowl or gave her treats and toys. She didn't sing. She didn't play. She stayed buried under mounds of timothy hay so you couldn't even see her. It was like having an empty cage that needed to be cleaned, fed and watered. I didn't get Eleanor a friend. I was pretty sure she had killed her last roomie, and I didn't want to do that to another poor soul. So I decided I had no choice but to just take care of Eleanor until she died. I mean, the other two had died within months (one within hours) of getting it, so how long could it really be? Well, Eleanor lived for four years. Four long, torturous, messy, smelly, painful years. And, on the day she died, the devil was officially out of a job.

Singing Frogs

When I met my husband he had two pets. One was a piranha I hated named Nozama, and the other was a fat smelly frog named Clyde. Erik's mom was a school teacher and Clyde had been a classroom pet that needed a place to go when school got out for the summer. So he went to Erik's house to live in a tiny dirty bowl. Now, keep in mind that Nozama the piranha was living in a one hundred gallon tank full of the most glorious and expensive décor that money could buy, being fed live goldfish ten times a day. He had two very expensive water filters and most importantly, he had love. Poor Clyde was an abandoned school project. He had no filter. He had no love. He was in a bowl so small he could barely move. His bowl smelled like the water that something dead has been soaking in for about six years. It was so cloudy you could barely see him through it. I was shocked. How could this wonderful man I was so in love with do this to a poor little frog?

So there was a week that Erik was going out of town for work so I was going to house sit for him. I realize now I should've spent this time trying to kill Nozama…but that would come later. I was going to surprise him with a whole new set up for the frog. Now, I don't know a thing about frogs. But, I know that if there is only one, there should probably be two. Everything gets lonely, right? Clyde needed a few friends. Now, I just wasn't sure where to get this type of frog. It wasn't a little frog and it wasn't a toad. It was just this thing that hung suspended in dirty water. If you fed him he jumped and grabbed the food with his creepy little hands and shoved it in his slimy mouth. Well, I did a little searching on the web and found a place that you could buy frogs like this on the internet. These frogs had been experimented on in a laboratory and were now for sale. This in my mind sort of seemed like "frog rescue" so I was on-board. I ordered four of them. Females. I was warned they may come with "issues" like missing limbs, grotesque malformed feet, glazed over or missing eyes...etc. Perfect! Right up my alley.

While I was waiting for the frogs to arrive via UPS, I set up a new tank for Clyde and his girlfriends. It was about a fifty gallon tank. I bought lots of décor for the tank to make it look like ancient Greece. Unfortunately, after doing some research, I discovered that you can't use a tank filter for frogs. Apparently the noise from the filter will make the frogs go insane and die. So, no filter. Just five frogs in a really big, heavy tank.

Midweek, the females arrived. I dumped them all in the tank with Clyde, added water and waited. Nothing happened. Which was good and bad. I mean, nobody killed anyone else, which was an improvement over the guinea pig situation. A few more days went by and Erik came home. I remember him pretending to be really happy about his new little frog family. I had put the frogs in his bedroom so he could enjoy them all the time. I hadn't really thought through about trying to sleep with the stench that frogs naturally make. Or maybe I did, and thought it would be incentive for Erik to take better care of them.

Then something miraculous happened. Clyde started to sing. He was singing for his girlfriends. He went from a disgusting dirty blob of slimy flesh into a singing frog! I loved singing Clyde. Erik loved singing Clyde. Clyde loved singing Clyde, and his ladies swooned. But alas, all good things must come to an end. First of all, I hadn't really thought out how Erik was going to clean out a fifty gallon tank every other day. You have to change the water frequently or it starts to smell. Really bad. This became a chore that was almost impossible. He did the best he could, but he was miserable. And then the frogs started to die.

I think most of the female frogs had some horrible illnesses from being experimented on in the lab. I have no idea how long a healthy frog lives, but these gals started dropping like flies. Within a few months all the females were dead and we were back to just Clyde. The smell, mess and time consuming task of cleaning the fifty gallon tank of death had gotten to everyone. So we popped Clyde back in his tiny bowl and waited. I mean, how long can a frog really live?

After Erik and I were married, Clyde moved in to our new house with us. He lived in a small bowl on the counter in the kitchen. He just hung there suspended in his dirty murky water and stunk. One day I got up and poked at him and he didn't move. He was dead! Finally! Glory be! Three years later and he was dead! When Erik woke up I told him Clyde was dead and he should do something with him. Erik went over to empty the bowl and when he did, Clyde jumped up trying to grab for his breakfast. From that day on, whenever I tell Erik something such as a fish, a rodent, or a dog has died, he makes me wait for him to get home before I do anything drastic with the remains; like burying them or putting them in the freezer.

Clyde lived another year after this. He lived in a tiny dirty bowl that nobody wanted to change. I silently cursed him every morning that he was still alive and stinking up the house. But I like to think back fondly of the days of Clyde swimming through Ancient Greece singing love songs to his ladies.

The Door Prize

When my son Oliver was about five years old we decided one weekend to go to the Reptile Show at the merchandise mart. You know, something inexpensive we could do as a family to kill the day. Besides, all little boys like reptiles, right? When you first walk in the door to the convention there was this table set up where the Boy Scouts were selling raffle tickets and giving away door prizes. I mean, it's the Boy Scouts, so you couldn't really say no. And the tickets were only twenty five cents each. Erik bought twelve tickets for the low, low price of three dollars. Unfortunately, you had to fill out each ticket with your name and phone number on the back, so Oliver and I went in to explore the show while Erik filled them out.

Personally, I had never been to a show like this before, but I presumed that it would be your typical reptile event. Lots of snakes, lots of lizards, and lots and lots of strange thirty-something men who live in their mother's basements, watch re-runs of Star Trek Deep Space 9 and sleep with their boas at night. The stereotypical reptile crowd…and I wasn't wrong.

I've got nothing against reptiles. I actually find them pretty fascinating. Erik has had a few lizards and iguanas in his lifetime. I thought this would be a good way to introduce Oliver to the world of herpetology. But here was the thing; it turns out that Oliver wasn't even remotely interested in the snakes, lizards or other cold-blooded creatures. He was interested in the mice. The mice that were scattered around the mart in various aquariums. The mice that were brought in as, well, lunch.

Oliver would run up to a booth of large boa constrictors squealing in delight, but he'd run right past the snakes and over to the feeder cages of mice. He was completely enamored. Erik and I were a bit perplexed. We certainly didn't want to scar him and ruin what was a perfectly nice day by telling him that the mice were for the snakes to eat.

I have to admit, I had been somewhat worried that Oliver would want to buy some super-expensive venomous snake, or some rare lizard that had to be hand fed live day old bunnies or something. But, no, he wanted some mice. So, we left the reptile convention and headed back home with a slight detour to Petsmart on the way. Oliver picked out three mice, all the same sex (or so we were told). We bought an aquarium, wheel, mouse house, you know, all the expensive Made in China junk mice couldn't care less about (as we would come to find out later in our lives).

Oliver was so happy. He had this new little mouse family to care for (which we all know means that I now had a little mouse family to care for). Anyway, we were driving home with our new mice when Erik got a phone call. It was from one of the Boy Scouts who had been at the raffle table. Seems we "need not be present to win" (thus the need for the name and phone number on the back of the ticket) and we had won something! Or, as it turns out, five something's. We won a book on corn snakes. We won a book on general herpetology. We won a reptile set-up that included "everything you need to make your reptile happy." And we won a money tree plant. Apparently, according to the Boy Scout that called Erik, by the time he had announced Erik's name for the third time, the crowd started to turn ugly. When they called Erik's name for the fourth time, people were mumbling about how the raffle was rigged. When Erik's name was announced for the fifth time, there was nearly a riot. We had won the Grand Prize! A snake. Yep. That's right. We had won some exotic, expensive snake. It was the size of a pencil, had a value of two hundred and twenty-five dollars and we needed to come and get it right now.

Well, Erik pulled over in to a gas station and we all just sat there in the car sort of stunned. A snake? After we had just bought a family of mice? Bummer. I didn't want a snake, but I don't hate them, either. I just don't like to feed pets to pets. Oliver was still oblivious to the fact that a snake eats mice. Erik sort of wanted the snake. I could tell. I can read him like a book. But, mostly, we were all in shock. And we had to make an instant decision. So, yes, we were going to go and get the snake. And all the other stuff we won.

To facilitate this, Erik had to take Oliver and I home so we could get our mice settled in their new home while he drove back to the convention to pick up our new snake. Looking back, I'm not sure why we didn't just say, "no thanks." Yes, we were in shock when we got the call saying that we won. And I guess when you finally win something, and it is the BIG GRAND PRIZE, you think you want it, even if you don't really want it.

Erik came home with this little pinkish grey snake in a Tupperware container. It was a good thing we had won a reptile set-up to go with the snake since we had just forked out a fortune for an aquarium for the mice. We couldn't have afforded to buy another. We put the snake in his cage on the opposite side of the house, far from Oliver's new mice. But soon the conversation of whether we should keep the snake or not came up. Because I didn't like the snake and Erik wanted to keep it, Erik did the only thing he could have done…he got Oliver involved. Even though Oliver didn't care about the snake one way or another, Erik had Oliver name it. If Oliver had a vested interest in it, there was no way I could ever get rid of it. Ever. Oliver named the snake PC, which stands for Pig Computer. Why? I don't know.

Years later, Pig Computer is still here with us. We've tried rehoming him, but nobody wants him. And, honestly, I think that Erik still really wants to keep him. But I am considering having my own reptile convention and dressing up as a Boy Scout so I can have a raffle and Pig Computer can be the GRAND PRIZE…for somebody else! Maybe even you.

What Evil Lurks...

I had gotten a call from the shelter about a little Lhasa Apso named Peanut. All they told me was that Peanut is about ten years old and that his owner had recently died. The son of the deceased woman took Peanut to the shelter because nobody in the family wanted him. Well, sadly, that's not out of the ordinary. Not an uncommon situation, for sure. Then the son told the shelter that Peanut was apparently not housebroken. There it was, the kiss of death for most dogs at the shelter, no matter their age. Of course, an old dog will have a more difficult time getting adopted, but if it isn't housebroken...well. Now, if the person surrendering the dog says something about the dog, the shelter has to disclose that information to potential adopters. A senior dog that wasn't housebroken? It certainly wasn't looking good for Peanut.

I agreed to take Peanut even though he is a bit on the younger side for our sanctuary. Ten really isn't that old for these smaller types of dogs, but I knew that the "not housebroken" comment had sealed his fate. Yeah, people are gonna' be coming to the shelter from the four corners of the earth and lining up at 3:00 a.m. for an opportunity to take Peanut home. Peanut was doomed. As doomed as doomed can be.

So I drove to the shelter to pick up Peanut. I've never had a Lhasa before, but my husband had them when he was younger and told me how sweet and smart and totally amazing they are. He considered himself an expert on the breed. He had Beau and Sheba, then he had Panda Bear. He was very fond of them. They were great companions, loved to go for walks, and were very loving. But, Erik also told me that the Lhasa was known as the "Lion Dog." Erik was wrong. In China, the Pekingese and the Shih Tzu are known as the "Lion Dog." The Lowchen is known as the "Little Lion" and will sometimes have their coat groomed to resemble a lion. The Rhodesian Ridgeback has also been known as VanRooyen's Lion Dog. But the Lhasa Apso, translated, is the "wolly Lhasa dog." Whatever that means. So much for my husband, the Lhasa expert. And so much for getting a dog that was anything like Beau, Sheba or Panda Bear.

When I first saw Peanut he certainly looked sweet. He was just a shaggy thing with tan fur and these big, bulging, watery eyes and his bangs were up in a pony-tail and tied with a green bow. He seemed very friendly and I got the leash on his collar with no problem and we walked out the front door and walked across the parking lot and got right in the car. It was obvious that he had been someone's pet, and it was obvious that his previous owner (or owners) had taken him for walks and that he liked walks. The person at the shelter told me a few things that I now see were clear foreshadowing of my future life with Peanut. The first thing is that Peanut had been alone in the house with his dead owner for "several days" and seemed pretty traumatized when arriving at the shelter. The second thing was that they had tried to groom him a bit for me at the shelter before I got there, but he "wasn't very cooperative." So they actually used a couple of phrases that should have immediately raised red flags for me. "Several days" and "wasn't very cooperative" are terms that are somewhat fluid and open to interpretation and can mean different things. "Several days" could be anywhere from two to eight. "Wasn't very cooperative" could mean everything from shaking nervously to going Cujo on everything in the room. Both of these terms leave out specific details that would come in handy in evaluating a dog.

But there was no turning back. Peanut had jumped with tremendous gusto into the car and decided he was coming home with me. Right now.

We had a very uneventful drive and I got Peanut back to the Sanctuary. He just seemed to me like a very sweet, well-adjusted dog. When we walked in the front door, he was pretty friendly with the other dogs and acted relieved to be in an actual home again. He introduced himself to the other dogs and got the lay of the land. He discovered that many of the dogs can't see or hear, and he realized that barking or bearing his teeth would have no effect on them. He found a bed to lay down on. He made a little nest in a bunch of blankets and rested for a few minutes. Then guess what he did next? He went to the front door and scratched on it. I let him out, he proceeded to go right to the grass, peed and then ran back inside. Hmmm. Now, I don't claim to be "Hope the Dog Whisperer" or "The Second Coming of Barbara Woodhouse," but in my experience, dogs that aren't housebroken don't really do that.

Of course, I'm very used to hearing things from the shelter that just aren't true, but they are usually good things about the dog that aren't true, not bad things that aren't true. I remember getting this chubby blind, deaf dachshund from a shelter, her name was Penelope. Among other lies, I was told that she could ring a bell when she needed to go potty. It was her signal to every human in the room that she needed to go outside. I presumed that it was some sort of mystic pseudo-Helen Keller "I am amazing" kind of thing, because some dogs are pretty amazing in what they can do, and didn't question it. After Penelope had been with us for a week, I came to the realization that I didn't know if her previous owners had some magical bell that could read Penelope's mind or if they were taking ecstasy or something, but Penelope's singular signal that she needed to go potty is that she would go potty on the floor in the living room and about half-way through she would look up at me as if to say "In case you didn't notice, I'm going potty right now." That was the signal. Pretty much a dollar short and a day late. I had bells all over the house for her, but she never got near a bell in any of her years with me. Ever. So the fantasy of a dog who would always let me know, in no uncertain terms, that they had to go potty, was dead. But, again, I am used to people lying to me about good things a dog can supposedly do. Not bad.

Anyway, I talked to the shelter a little more in depth about Peanut and the son had said when they discovered his mom (who he said had been dead for the ambiguous "a few days") he noticed that there was dog pee and poop all over the house. Well, I don't know how long the son thought Peanut could hold it with no access to the outdoors but this led him to believe that Peanut was not housebroken. Even our most normal dog can't go more than a full day. It's just not possible, even under the best of circumstances. And it can't be healthy to hold it for that long, either.

So the first few days went okay. Peanut liked being upstairs and would let me lift him on and off of the couch. He would stiffen up and get very tense when I picked him up, which I thought was a little odd, but he let me do it. This was our honeymoon period. I would pick him up and he wouldn't kill me. It's a simple premise. Pick up. No bite. Put down. Still no bite. I reflect back fondly on those days.

I can't exactly remember when Peanut started doing his Jekyll and Hyde routine. Peanut is one of the friendliest dogs I've ever had. He loves to play with the other dogs, he loves to sit on your lap and sometimes he'll just stand in the middle of the room and wag his tail and smile. I can kiss his squishy little mouth, rub his belly, and scratch behind his ears. But after about a three day break in period, I couldn't pick him up. I couldn't brush him or attempt to groom him in any way. I couldn't trim his nails. Peanut just turns quickly into a snapping ball of fury; all teeth and bitter anger. And he has this crazy look in his eyes. And even after I stopped doing whatever it was that made him want to kill me, he'd keep going. And going. And going and going and going. He'd chase me down long after the fact, just to make sure I understood he didn't like that. But then after a few minutes he would be so apologetic. He would come stand up on my leg, lick me and wag his tail, just like nothing had happened.

Peanut being a Lhasa Apso presents two major issues. One is that he needs to be groomed on a fairly regular basis. Two is that Lhasa Apsos don't have snouts that you can muzzle. Because we are a small sanctuary and run on a tight budget, we typically do our own grooming. We invested in a really good set of clippers that get the job done pretty quickly. Since we don't have the talent to do an extraordinary job we just do a full shave and at least it's over fast. Hey, it isn't pretty but it is free, so it works for us. And for the dog.

But we found out with Peanut that even with the best clippers in the world, home grooming just isn't possible. And we also discovered, much to our chagrin, that taking Peanut to the groomer was also not an option. Oh no. He wasn't any happier about someone else grooming him than he was with us doing the job. So here is the routine. We let Peanut's grooming go as long as possible. The hair starts to cover his eyes which makes him turn into this evil gatekeeper of sorts. He'll lay in the doorway of the most trafficked area in our house and pretend to be sleeping. Now keep in mind, most of our dogs are partially, if not completely blind, so they don't even see him lying there. Then he proceeds to attack every dog that gets within two feet of his blurry-by-hair vision. He just sort of jumps out at them and retracts like a Moray eel hunting from a hole in a coral reef. Except that Peanut's teeth are probably a little bit sharper. This is our cue that it is time for a grooming.

We have to take Peanut to the vet, where he has to be completely knocked out and shaved. Yep. It costs us around two hundred dollars each time we do it. The only great thing about this arrangement is that when we pick him up from the vet he is too groggy to try to kill us. He is still coming out of anesthesia so we can do whatever we want to him. So we make a big production out of carrying him around like a baby wrapped in a blanket and we kiss him, hold him, and dress him up like a ballerina. All the things he would never let us do if he weren't so drugged. Oh, and the first time we had this done the vet informed us that Peanut is more like seven years old. Seven years old and housebroken. Certainly adoptable, just based on those terms. But the fact that he is schizophrenic and extremely violent? Is he still adoptable now? Not so much. So I guess he ended up in the right place, after all.

It averages out that we have to take Peanut to the vet to get shaved every three months. The first few times we tried to transport him, it took a long time to catch him and the drive was pretty dangerous. But now we have a routine. We corner him, toss a blanket over his head and get his harness and leash on him. We can do this in eight seconds or less. It's like we are doing the Peanut Rodeo. Once we have him harnessed up, he can lunge and try to bite as much as he wants, but we are in control of how far his mouth can reach. Peanut has also learned that being in the car means he is going to the vet. So once we get him in the car, he becomes slightly more docile purely out of fear. But only slightly. Once we are at the vet and get him through the front door, as far as I'm concerned, he's their problem. They know he bites. And they know how to deal with it. They sedate the heck out of him. When completely drugged, he is just like a normal dog. Except, of course, that his eyes are sort of crossed and if you put him down, he just sort of stands there swaying. But he only has one personality. And it is the good one.

A few times, as you inevitably will with this breed of dog, we have had some emergency butt shaving sessions with Peanut. If you have a dog that requires grooming I'm sure you're familiar with this nasty chore. With most dogs it isn't a big deal but with Peanut, well I'm sure you can imagine the fun had by all. There was one time that was particularly horrifying.

We noticed Peanut's butt was all blocked up and he was very uncomfortable. It was a Sunday evening, so we knew we had no choice but to either take Peanut to the emergency vet (which is forty minutes away, and they certainly wouldn't have seen this as an "emergency") or wait to take him to our vet in the morning (and have Peanut suffer all night long) or try to remedy the situation ourselves. Well, we are pretty pro-active at the Sanctuary. So, first, we threw a blanket over Peanut's head. Second, we tackled him. He may be a small dog, but he is strong. Like Regan in The Exorcist.

After we both had hands securely on him, we quickly put him up on the kitchen counter. Erik held him and I was shaving him as fast as I could. But about twenty seconds in to the procedure, he slithered out of Erik's grip and got his head out from under the blanket. He then proceeded to bite my husband on the hand, right in that area between his left thumb and forefinger. And he bit it hard.

Now, my husband is a very undemonstrative person. You have to know him really well to discern what each look of his means. He only has about five of them. His expression remains pretty much the same in each look, but he will do something subtle like lift one eyebrow or cock his head to the side. He is a quiet guy, not easily ruffled. Well, he dropped Peanut to the floor and kicked the cabinet door and then leaned over the sink and didn't move a muscle or say a word for fifteen minutes. I took this to mean that he was hurt. I have only seen this kind of emotion from my husband three times in our marriage. When the Broncos lost in the Superbowl to the Seattle Seahawks, when the Avalanche blew the Stanley Cup playoffs and now with Peanut almost taking his thumb off. I knew that it had to be serious.

After Erik had regained some use of his hand we tried again and this time were successful. And you know what? Erik was actually worried that the struggle had somehow hurt Peanut. Yep, he was worried about Peanut. I'm telling you, I married the most perfect man in the world. I'm sure the fifteen minutes of silence he displayed after the attack was spent envisioning every possible way he could murder Peanut and quite possibly me, since it was initially me who stole him from his blissful, bachelor existence and brought him to this surreal life where he was being attacked by a vicious Lhasa Apso while trying to shave his poopy butt, but I loved that he was worried about Peanut afterwards. Erik still has the scars from this event and he has limited use of his left thumb and forefinger. Just ask him to see the scars, he'll be happy to show them to you. And he will tell you, with pride, that any time we have an emergency butt shaving situation with Peanut, he now wears welding gloves. And they work great.

The sad thing about Peanut is that after he displays this kind of aggressive behavior, he is very apologetic. Well, not immediately. After you put him down from an emergency shaving, he'll jump up and try to bite you a few more times. But then the switch flips. The vacant, crazy look in his eyes disappears and you can see into his loving, kind, caring soul. Then he's sorry. He'll come stand up on your leg and wag his tail and want kisses. When he displays this side of his personality, it is extremely difficult to be angry with him.

Besides the most amazing Jekyll and Hyde act you could imagine, Peanut has another talent. Now every dog has a talent. Or a redeeming trait or fascinating quality. Just like with people. Everybody has something. But Peanut has two things.

I wish that I could say that Peanut has an amazing talent worthy of his own TV show on the Discovery Channel. I wish I could say that he followed a toddler as he wandered away from home and into the woods and protected said toddler from wolves and bears and Bigfoot until said toddler was rescued by the thankful town-folk. I wish I could say that Peanut was a dedicated service dog who refused to leave the grave of his owner, rain or shine. I wish I could say that Peanut alerted an entire nursing home to a fire and evacuated everyone before the entire home burned to the ground. Heck. I wish I could say that Peanut was able to find bedbugs. But he can't. So there will be no TV show. There is no sugar-coating Peanut's other talent. And we discovered it because of Norman.

Norman is a twenty-one-year-old terrier that came to us from California. When we got him, his coat was patchy and disgusting, and he had some skin disorder that made sections of him look like a reptile that's allergic to shellfish after it just ate twenty pounds of shrimp that had been sitting out in the hot sun for three days. Not good. Not good at all. It looked like he died way back in 1977 with Joan Crawford, the Indian Motorcycle Company, and Disco, but was lingering around mortal earth. Just for kicks.

But we de-wormed Norman and stopped using the wickedly expensive shampoos and lotions that traveled along with him from

California and a month later he was unrecognizable. Beautiful flowing hair, clear eyes, and an insatiable appetite. He is always wagging his tail, and is an expert at mistiming jumps from the yard onto the back deck. But there is one thing about Norman that we didn't know until Peanut pointed it out to us.

Erik and I were standing in the kitchen making dinner one evening when we saw Peanut walk up to Norman and start licking his neck. Norman started wagging his tail. And Peanut was wagging his tail. It seemed like a regular love-fest.

"That's nice," we said, because Peanut didn't really have any other dogs that he had bonded with, and most of the dogs here have at least one "buddy" to hang out with, snuggle, or play with. And we talked about how we wished that some of Norman's wonderful personality could rub off on Peanut so that maybe, someday, he wouldn't go crazy and attack us anymore. We went about making dinner and Peanut kept licking Norman's neck. Five minutes went by. Then ten. Finally, I pulled Peanut away from Norman and saw that Norman had a lump on his neck, and it was bleeding.

That is when we discovered that Peanut loves blood. And I don't mean in a curious, scientific sort of way. No. He loves blood in a Count Orlok meets Jaws in the never-made movie Nosferatu Jaws sort of way. Incidentally, Peanut has two rows of teeth in his mouth…so the shark thing is quite possible. But, you know, this is Little Old Dog Sanctuary, so anything is possible.

Yeah, it's kind of gross. But at our house, his skill comes in quite handy. First of all, if you have an old dog, you understand about the lumps and bumps they have on their bodies and that they can bleed. Peanut is the first to alert us about any bleeding wound on any dog. If there has been some kind of fight we didn't witness, Peanut alerts us where to check for a wound. There are times I would have never noticed an issue if I didn't see Peanut following that dog around licking it. Secondly, we never have to clean up blood from the floor or blankets, Peanut takes care of that for us.

The only thing is, he always looks up at us like he just finished the appetizer, "so now where's the main course?"

I don't want to believe that Peanut's skill is as a direct result from when his owner died. The thought of Peanut having to survive by drinking his owner's blood and/or eating her is a little too much to bear. But, as with all of our dogs, we can't change their past. All we can give them is the present. And, in Peanut's case his present is a little blood now and then. At the Sanctuary, we do what we can.

Greener Acres

Things were going well with our little farm. Everyone was getting along. There was structure and routine. The sociological, ecological and psychological aspects of the barnyard were ticking right along like clockwork. Smooth as silk. Perfect. So, obviously, it was time for me to do something, shake things up a little bit. I have never left well enough alone.

I was looking on PineCam (a local sort of Craigslist) and saw that there was a goat nearby that needed a new home. I jumped on it immediately. I mean, we had two cute goats who were hardly any work at all. Now looking back, I should've realized I was tempting fate. But, as usual, my decision to get another goat was based on what I currently had, which is never a good way to make a decision, especially about goats. I gave Erik the phone number and address and instructed him to go and rescue the goat.

The people who had the goat lived in the mountains, not too far from our home. They told Erik that they had started with about a dozen goats, but they were down to one. Now, I'm no math wizard, but that is eleven goats unaccounted for. What happened to the others? Well, the goats lived on these people's property but had no shelter of their own. They were fenced in by a small, wire fence that was only three feet tall. You could climb right over it (or through it, for that matter) if you wanted to. Now leaving a dozen goats outside in the mountains with no shelter and mediocre protective fencing is sort of like feeding the wildlife. Well, there's nothing "sort of" about it. It is feeding the wildlife. But not the birds, squirrels or the deer. It's more of a buffet for the bears, mountain lions and coyotes. And, eventually, the vultures. Here's some goat canapés…come and get it! And get it, they did. And then some. And then some more.

Now, maybe it's just me, but I would have thought about either creating a safer environment or rehoming the goats when one went missing. Or certainly after two went missing. But deciding to take action when there was only one left? You might just as well let the mountain lion, coyotes or bears have it at that point.

Erik stuffed the lone survivor into the car and brought her home. We named her Lola. Now Lola wasn't a pygmy goat like Gus and Petunia. She was your standard variety petting zoo goat. She is big, obnoxious, and pushy and has huge horns (unlike the unfortunate Gus and Petunia). And she's crazy. Not just regular goat crazy, but, "I've been outside watching my friends get taken away every night by large meat-eating predators" kind of crazy. She is also an attention hog. She wants all the attention all the time. ALL THE TIME. And if she doesn't get it? She'll bite you, butt you, steal whatever you are holding in your hands, rip your clothing, or jump up with her feet on your shoulders. And if she doesn't have your complete attention because you are giving it to someone else, she will drive that "someone else" away really, really fast. Even if you are talking on your cell phone. She'll knock it right out of your hand. She hates competition and is smart enough to know that the best way to conquer the competition is to get rid of it.

Gus and Petunia have always been a bit standoffish of us…shy, timid and afraid of everything. They wouldn't come out of the coop when it was raining because they were afraid of rain. They were afraid of birds. Not like "here comes a giant hawk to eat someone," but like hummingbirds. And sparrows. And chickens. Whom they live with. Not good. Lola is like the anti-Gus and Petunia. She is only afraid of being eaten at night by something very large. That is about it. So, the one good thing about Lola is that she taught Gus and Petunia that the world isn't so scary. That mud really isn't all that frightening, that rain won't kill you and the chickens probably won't either. And, as a matter of fact, if you let the chickens sit on your back, they will eat the deer flies while giving you a deep tissue massage.

Spending time outside with the chickens and little goats used to be such a pleasant experience. It was like a magical, metaphysical meditation. It was like a yoga and valium smoothie. Super-sized. With a cherry on top. But after Cornelius started plotting my murder it lost some of its Zen-like qualities. My yoga and valium smoothie quickly spoiled in the sun and was now teeming with bacteria and dirt. But I could live with it. Now add Lola to the mix and visiting the chicken run was more like taking crabby toddlers hopped up on pixie sticks to the Water World Amusement Park on the fourth of July in a lightning storm on Hells Angels Appreciation Day. Not relaxing. Not relaxing, at all.

Lola immediately rushes you when you walk into the run. She pushes her head into whatever you might be carrying. If you have food she'll rip it out of your hands. If you have a coat on, she'll try to get in your pockets. She'll trample the chickens to get to you first. If you are trying to give attention to anything or anyone else she'll nip at you from behind. She's strong, pushy and mean. And she is madly in love with Gus and hates Petunia.

Gus and Petunia came from the same farm. They aren't brother and sister, but they have been together since they were babies. Gus is pretty friendly, but Petunia is shy. If only because of their history, Gus loves Petunia. And that makes Lola mad. And it makes her hate Petunia even more. Petunia is small, beautiful and delicate. Lola is big, bossy, mean and jealous. She routinely blocks the door of the coop so Petunia has to stay outside in the rain, hail, snow, sub-freezing temperatures and darkness. She chases Petunia off so you can't give her any treats. She commands all of Gus' attention. But no matter what she does, Gus still loves Petunia. Unrequited love; it just makes Lola even crazier.

Well, I am the type of person who is pretty committed to whatever kind of mess I happen to get myself into, so I figured I had to just deal with Lola much in the same way I dealt with Cornelius. She was just being a goat, and I didn't really blame her for being so crazy...you'd be crazy too if something came into your house every night and ate eleven of your siblings.

One day I came home from the grocery store and happened to glance out at the chicken run and saw something very strange. It looked like a giant bug wrapped in a spider's web. Like a cocoon of sorts. I realized with horror that it was Lola. Somehow she had gotten wrapped up in the aviary netting that covers the top of the chicken run. She must have gotten a piece of it stuck in her horns, panicked and tore it all down by running. This is really strong netting, so it doesn't rip easily. She was stuck.

I ran in to the run thinking Lola was dead, but she wasn't. Not yet. She was sweating profusely and couldn't even move. Her mouth was bound shut, I could just see one of her eyes. She was so tightly wound up in that netting I couldn't get it to budge. I ran inside and got the scissors. I ran out and just started cutting around Lola's face and neck area. Yes, there are times in life when it is okay to run with scissors. And this was one of them, if I've ever seen it.

I got her mouth free and she bit me. The more netting I cut and the more she could move the more she would get herself tangled up. I got her front legs free, so she started kicking me. She kicked so much she got trapped in the netting again. After about forty five minutes I finally freed her. She ran around stumbling like she was drunk, but eventually stabilized. I now realized I was covered in mud, goat urine, chicken poop and blood (from her kicking and biting me). My dress was ripped and I had so much adrenaline rushing through my body I thought I was going to vomit. But Lola was alive, and as much as I hated her, I also loved

119

her and was glad she was alive. But now she was traumatized...again. And adding yet another stressful and near death experience didn't help her disposition at all.

After a few days of everyone in the run being a little on edge, they all sort of picked up where they left off and life went on. We added more chickens to our flock. Some we rescued, some we bought. We were getting two dozen useless eggs a day. Cornelius was still attacking me. Lola was still obnoxious. This is when we decided how fun it would be to have turkeys.

We had read several things saying turkeys and chickens can't live together. There is something called "blackhead" that chickens can give turkeys. They transmit it in their poop, it is fatal and can live in a dormant state in the ground for years and years and years. But we had also read a lot of things saying that, yes, you can keep turkeys and chickens together. And, having visited at least a dozen farms since we began ours, there isn't a single instance where we saw that the turkeys and chickens were segregated. Everything lived together. After a brief conversation, Erik and I threw caution to the wind and we decided to give it a try.

Now you have to understand we are vegetarians over here. We weren't planning on eating the turkeys, we wanted them as pets. Most turkeys are bred for meat, so they are huge. Most turkey meat you get from the store is from turkeys that grow so huge that they can't even walk. Well, we have enough dogs that have difficulty walking, so this wasn't what we were looking for. Instead, we decided to get a heritage breed, the Royal Palm. The Royal Palm is small for a turkey, weighing in at around twenty pounds or so, yet they still seem huge. Especially compared to the chickens. They are not aggressive, the hens make good mothers, and, visually, the Royal Palm is just flat-out striking. Stunning, even, which is interesting because they are only a couple of colors. Other than the red on their heads and necks, they are mostly white with metallic black markings. Sadly, they are currently considered to be "very endangered," so that was even more reason for us to get some.

We got three Toms and one hen. I think I told Erik we wanted three hens and one Tom and he misunderstood. When he got them home they looked just like baby chicks. We couldn't tell the difference between the sexes. We put them in with our other baby chicks and we honestly couldn't discern who was a chicken and who was a turkey. That issue lasted for about two days. Then the turkeys started growing at an alarming rate. At least three times as fast as the chickens. It was ridiculous. We had them living in the baby chick nursery in the garage, but it wasn't long before they were big and strong enough to start roosting on the sides of the pen. And they were not particularly friendly. And, unlike what we'd read, they were much more nervous than the chickens. And very suspicious. I guess they had heard rumors about Thanksgiving and all.

Roosting on the sides of the pen indicates to us that they were almost ready to go out into the coop. And, a week later, they were more than ready to go. It turned out that moving the turkeys out to the coop from the garage was quite an event. The turkeys were enormous. And strong. And they didn't like us. So this wasn't going to be easy. And since the garage contains a hoard of epic proportions, maneuvering around the stuff intended to be sold off at a garage sale we've been planning on having for six years with a large and extremely freaked out bird sounded hazardous on many levels.

In keeping with expectations, the first one we grabbed totally freaked out. I guess when they are born they just know to hit you in the face with their wings. It is a really effective defense. The closest thing I can compare it to is like being hit in the face with a broom. Really, really hard. And often. It blinds you and injures you at the same time. After about five seconds of this, you are certainly ready to put them down. But if you can get your arms around their wings and keep your eyes away from their beaks (lest they peck them out) it is a lot easier to carry them. I guess they didn't know we were taking them outside to a turkey nirvana. They probably thought we were going to introduce them to the mashed potatoes and pumpkin pie in a 350 degree Fahrenheit sauna.

So we caught and hauled three out to the coop and were left with Hedda. It was neither an accident nor chance that Hedda was the last one to be moved. She's the only hen and she's mean and crazy. In and of itself, mean and crazy is not out of our comfort zone. We've had plenty of animals up here that are mean and crazy. For most of them, they just act this way when they first arrive, then they settle down. But some of them stay that way forever, and that is okay. Again. We're used to it. It's not a big deal. But here is the thing about turkeys, and why they were on a whole new level for us. Turkeys can fly. Chickens can't really fly. I mean, they make half-hearted attempts, but it is more a long "jump" than actual flying, much like Walter trying to jump on the couch. An incredible and epic effort immediately followed by equally incredible and epic failure.

Now, in all fairness, technically, chickens fly. I've seen a chicken fly. And they get about three feet off the ground and maybe they'll go twenty feet or so before they come back down to terra firma. But usually, they can't even do this. Chickens are like the Wright Brothers and turkeys are Boeing. Chickens are so much better at running, they stick with their strengths. Watching a chicken run is really cool. It is like watching a tiny dinosaur with feathers. But it's not fun to watch if you actually need to catch it. Do you need to get in to great physical shape? Do you need to lose some weight? Do you need to fight Apollo Creed for the Heavyweight Title of the World? Try to catch a chicken that doesn't want to be caught. That scene from Rocky 2 isn't make believe. But I digress.

Just like with every animal, whenever there is a strength, there is also a weakness. Turkeys can fly, but they are not very smart. Conversely, if you think a chicken is stupid, think again. A turkey makes a chicken look like Einstein. Well, of course, Hedda decided to fly in order to escape our grasp. She took off (keep in mind, the garage has so much crap in it that there is only about two feet at the very top of the ceiling that isn't blocked). Hedda flew up and over to the other side of the garage and flew into the wall going full speed. I thought she had probably given herself a mild concussion and that we might be able to grab her, but no luck. She fell behind a huge stack of boxes and disappeared. After digging for an hour we finally found her and she was totally exhausted and so were we. But we got her out into the run, and that was that. Had we tried moving Hedda before the Tom's, the Tom's would still probably be living in the garage. We would have simply given up.

I'm sure you're thinking that I made a bad choice by adding the turkeys. Not at all. They were finally old enough to do what I got them for...they were ready to give us the grand payoff. And I have to admit, having my very own turkey "puff up" into the classic "turkey shape" while doing the whole "gobble gobble" thing is more exciting than I ever could have imagined. And this group does it all the time. They are excellent guard birds. Most of the time, I hear them warn of predators before I hear our Great Pyrenees. They are very vocal.

But, again, they aren't the shiniest apples in the barrel. So, because of their tiny brains, they get stuck out in the storms...rain, hail and snow. They also usually can't figure out how to get back into the coop at night, so we have to put them back in. No wonder they are "very endangered." Luckily, once the sun goes down, they turn into turkey statues so there isn't much of a problem in catching them and depositing them into the coop. And watching them puff up and gobble and strut around in perfect formation makes all of the hassle worth it.

After a few months, things had settled down a bit. The turkeys, chickens and goats were living in harmony. Well, for the most part. But the universe must have been made aware of our relative calm because I got an email from a fellow dog rescuer who had accidently gotten a rooster and couldn't keep him (she lived in Denver where you can only have hens). They loved the rooster and wanted to make sure he ended up somewhere as a pet and not as hot wings. Re-homing a rooster is complicated on a few levels, but we love a challenge, so we agreed to take him. His name was Mr. B. Mr. B had two problems. One, he is a rooster and we already have roosters. Roosters don't get along. Two, Mr. B is a bantam, which is a reference to size and all it means is that he is a small chicken. And that means that Mr. B could not only get beaten up and killed by the roosters, but also by any of the hens. Or a chipmunk, for that matter.

When they brought Mr. B over, we put him in the chicken run and he did fine for about five minutes. Then the turkeys noticed him. The thing about turkeys is that they have about a million strange behaviors that I'm assuming all mean something to them, but are confusing to me. Well, when they saw Mr. B they quickly formed into a "turkey gang." They were bunched up into a tight group with Hedda in the lead. The toms were puffed up making their turkey sounds. They were dragging the tips of their wings on the ground which makes this ominous loud scraping sound. They would move as a bunch in a tight "V" formation and started stalking Mr. B. I mean, they were relentless. They weren't really doing anything other than being really strange and intimidating but Mr. B looked so tiny and I felt bad for him having to endure the newly formed turkey gang. The turkey's behavior was so strange it caught the attention of Cornelius who then noticed Mr. B, so there began the rooster fighting. Now, when you add a new chicken to the flock they have to reestablish the whole pecking order. You have to just sort of let them fight it out. Separating them just prolongs this redistribution of power. But Mr. B was getting the crap beat out of him by Cornelius who was about three times his size. I tried putting Mr. B in the coop but that was far worse. Not wanting Mr. B to get killed on his first night here, or ever, I brought him inside and put him in a wire dog cage in the "no dog zone." Which, technically, was fine. He's a bird, not a dog.

My dogs are pretty used to crazy things and didn't pay much attention to Mr. B. And Mr. B seemed to like it there much better than outside. So he lived in the house until I could figure out what to do with him. I have to say, waking up to a rooster crowing in your living room is pretty awesome. I loved it. If I could figure out how to keep a rooster indoors all the time, I would. I half considered just letting Mr. B be my indoor rooster, but I was worried at some point one of the dogs would realize that they could eat Mr. B, and I didn't want that to happen. So, we set up a chicken pen in the garage and I went outside and got some of the hens that were low in the pecking order and getting picked on. They became Mr. B's little haram. They all lived in harmony in the garage. But they couldn't stay there forever. It was too small of a space and the garage gets hot in the summer and cold in the winter. After trying a few things to no avail, I contacted the original owner of Mr. B and told her that it wasn't going to work out.

Mr. B's original owner was sad. I was sad. Mr. B was sad. Mr. B's haram was sad. But then guess what happened? World Peace came to the Sanctuary.

I get a lot of emails from a lot of people about animals in need, but this is the first time I'd ever gotten one like this. It was about a pig that needed a new home. The pig was living on a mini-farm in Denver. In the County of Denver, you can have a few chickens and a goat, but no pigs. The owners got busted by animal control and they had no idea what to do with the pig. They were worried, rightfully so, that he was going to end up as breakfast. I have always wanted a pig. Always. This was a mini potbellied pig. Not too mini, though. His name was World Peace. They sent me pictures of him with their daughter riding on his back - World Peace didn't look too thrilled. Anyway, it was near our wedding anniversary so I thought this would be a good gift from Erik to me, though I'm sure he would have preferred to get me flowers.

When I heard World Peace was living on a mini farm in Denver, I thought that maybe he was living on the outskirts of the city or perhaps in an industrial area by the railroad tracks. Nope. World Peace lived in a run-down neighborhood in a somewhat sketchy part of town that was only a few blocks away from Mile High Stadium and downtown. He lived just a few houses down from a really busy street. His only shelter was a hole that he burrowed beneath the house. Erik said that he couldn't hear World Peace "oink" over the sound of the traffic.

The family that had World Peace was very nice, and they realized that maybe they were in a little over their head by having

125

him there. He loved to dig massive holes in the dirt and eat the chicken eggs. Erik could believe the egg thing as it took three people to lift World Peace into the back of his Ford Bronco. All that Erik would say about the drive home was that it was "interesting" and in the same breath he mentioned that "maybe we should consider investing in a livestock trailer."

I remember the first time I saw World Peace. He was so beautiful. The first thing I noticed were his long, lovely eyelashes. And then he snorted, I almost burst from joy! An actual pig snort! It was music to my ears. I fed him lots of treats before he ever got out of the car. Carrots, cereal, muffins. We bonded. Then Erik explained how World Peace didn't want to get in the car. And then we both discovered that the only thing he hated more than getting in the car was getting out of the car. And he was about one hundred and fifty pounds of squirming stubbornness at this point, so lifting him out with just the two of us wasn't an option. We fashioned a leash and collar out of a soft piece of rope and made a ramp out of a long piece of wood. I lured him down the ramp and all the way into the chicken run with cereal. The goats were mortified. World Peace seemed pleased. He explored the whole area, wagging his pig-tail and making happy snorting noises.

I changed his name from World Peace to Roy because, well, c'mon. Roy seemed more appropriate. Good Boy Roy.

Roy was just a joy to have around. He loved it here immediately. We set him up a little bed area in the coop and he was just in heaven. Pigs are smart, and Roy figured out the routine almost immediately. Truth be told, Roy is smarter than most of the dogs we have. He can "sit" on command, which he will gladly do for his favorite thing…peanut butter. He knows his name and comes running when you call him. He's a sweet guy. And the whole vibe of the barnyard area changed overnight.

On a hunch, we decided to give it one more go with Mr. B out with the general population in the chicken run. And the most amazing thing happened. We put him out there and he was fine. No fighting from the roosters and hens, no parading and grandstanding from the turkeys...nothing. Nothing at all. The turkey gang had dispersed back into four individual turkeys. Cornelius had gone back to picking on me instead of Mr. B. Even Mr. B's haram of hens weren't getting picked on anymore.

It was no secret what had happened. Roy happened. Roy doesn't tolerate bullying and Roy doesn't tolerate fighting. And he's big enough to back it up. When Roy appeared, the fighting and animosity just stopped. Well, except for one thing. Cute, shy, little Petunia spends her days sneaking up behind Roy and butting him right in the rear end every chance she gets! Roy doesn't dignify her actions with a response. Yes, Roy is that classy.

So things are back to normal at the Sanctuary. Our new normal. Everyone has settled in and is living in harmony. And harmony among the animals gives me extra time to think. I wonder how an old cow would do at the Sanctuary?

The Best Dog in the World

Melvin is one of those "once in a lifetime" type of dogs. I am sure that if you saw him at a shelter or on the street you wouldn't think he was anything special. You'd see a brown dog that was not too big and not too small. You would hear a bark that was not too loud and not too soft. You would see a dog that was too big to be a lap dog and too small to be a guard dog. You'd get all the "just right" stuff from the Goldilocks and the Three Bears story, and that would be fine if you were looking for porridge or a bed or something. But it certainly would not be impressive. It would not be flashy. You would think that Melvin is just average and run of the mill. Maybe even boring. You would judge a book by its cover. And you'd be wrong. Totally, 110 percent wrong.

If you took a minute to get to know him, you'd realize that negative energy just shrivels up and dies when Melvin licks you on the hand. Something about Melvin just makes you feel happy. He has this amazing vibe that can fill a room with rainbows and unicorns. Some way, somehow, Melvin's love and energy that radiates from his soul can pierce even the deepest and harshest of hurt, anger and despair. His love is better than the usual unconditional love that accompanies the presence of most dogs. Melvin offers a love that transcends all, and can carry you from this lifetime clear through to the next one. Melvin was, is, and always will be, without a doubt, "The Best Dog in the World."

I got Melvin from a county shelter where his owners dumped him at the age of sixteen. They said they didn't have time for him anymore. Call me naïve, but I guess I don't know what this means. He's sixteen, how much time could he possibly need? He eats. He sleeps. He poops. He sleeps some more. And then he wakes up and starts over again. He is not demanding in any way whatsoever. He is perfect. He is willing to take how much or how little anybody has to offer with no questions asked and no determination of expectations met or unfulfilled. Depending on the need at the time, he can be very social or he can be self-contained and self-sustaining. We're not completely sure, but we think that he can use his dew claw as an opposable thumb, therefore giving him the ability to use a can opener and drive a car. Again, he was, is, and will always be, without a doubt, "The Best Dog in the World."

Melvin's owners had gotten him as a baby. I have paperwork from day one of his birth until he got dumped. They surrendered a file containing every vet record and grooming receipt from the past sixteen years of his life. That shows effort, organization, attention to detail and that they cared enough to make sure that the physical condition of the dog is well-maintained. Those are certainly some attributes associated with a good pet owner. Now, dumping a dog you've had for sixteen years at a high-kill county shelter because he is getting too old to go for a three mile jog every morning and because he accidently peed on the carpet last week are not attributes of a good pet owner. Not at all. And to top it all off, when they were leaving the shelter, they made mention of buying a new puppy on the way home. People suck. If you believe in Hell, there is surely a section labeled, "I'm here because I dumped my old dog at the shelter." These are the same kinds of people who dump their parents in shoddy nursing homes. Running the Sanctuary reminds me on a daily basis why I generally prefer the company of animals over the company of people. And I always will.

Now, I am a good judge of animals, and I knew right off the bat that Melvin was something special. But, wanting to still believe in humanity, I kept thinking I would soon discover the real reason his family took him to the shelter. I mean, nobody in their right mind would dump a perfectly good dog to be killed. Would they? People can say whatever they want, but usually it quickly becomes apparent why a dog like Melvin has ended up at the shelter. Does he have accidents in the house? Does he have dementia? Does he bark nonstop? Does he have a gambling problem? Is he aggressive with other dogs? Is he aggressive with other dogs while gambling?

But as each day passed I only discovered reasons why I, and why anybody in their right mind, would want to keep Melvin. He is sweet. I mean, pixie stick, lollypop, Lemonade Peeps covered in chocolate kind of sweet. He is relaxed and doesn't get riled up about anything. He is easy to please and wags his tail constantly. He loves to be brushed and we never have any issues when it is time to clip his nails. Please refer to the chapter on Peanut to see Melvin's alter-ego when it comes to grooming. But all Melvin requires is a bed, some food and love. And then there was the biggest surprise of all...he is housebroken! Imagine that.

Melvin didn't seem to miss his old family too much and settled right in. He was one of the few dogs we could actually take places. I remember one day we took Melvin (who is a thirty pound mutt) and our tiny, gorgeous, breed standard and magazine cover perfect looking three pound Chihuahua, Chester Von Wee Wee, to the pet store. Now every little girl within fifty miles was lining up to pet Chester. Chester is very cute. His fur is so fine he looks naked. He was wearing a tiny adorable sweater. He has big, watery eyes that look like they will pop out of his head and he shakes non-stop. If you go and look in Merriam Webster right now, you will see a photo of Chester under the word "Adorable." And that would be accurate. However, this would again be a case of making a horrible mistake by judging a book by its cover.

Here's the thing, Chester is mean. Like, bite your fingers off and then swallow-them "just to teach you a lesson" sort of mean.

Attack your face with razor sharp teeth and rip it off in a frenzied, nearly rabid Chimpanzee-style mean. Those little girls were in for the shock of their life when they reached for tiny Chester. Their initial image of Chester was destroyed and their hearts were broken. But here was Melvin. Wagging his tail, staring up at people with his love-radiating eyes. But nobody wanted to pet Melvin. He wasn't tiny and naked except for an adorable sweater. He wasn't shaking nonstop. His eyes didn't look like they were going to pop out of his head. And, sadly, for a lot of people, that just doesn't do it for them.

Typically our dogs are too old, too ill, too crazy or all of the above to take out in public. Needless to say, Melvin became a staple for walks and public appearances and other "Sanctuary Sponsored" activities of a social nature. He was a little deaf and a little blind, but that didn't matter. He could get by, wasn't frightened, and his legs were in good working order. We were overjoyed that we finally had a dog that we could take out in public!

So, with tremendous pride, we took Melvin to an outdoor festival we visit each year. It was fall, the festival was Cider Days at the Heritage Arts and Culture Center, the air was cool and crisp, and there were thousands of people milling about enjoying music, food and fun. Melvin loved it! He wagged his tail the whole time. When we first walked through the gate, there was this little girl who spotted Melvin. She was with her Grandmother, who was obviously not a dog lover. But she couldn't keep this little girl away from Melvin, she was smitten. She ran over and threw her arms around Melvin's neck like she had known him forever. Melvin has that effect of people. We call it "The Melvin Effect."

Her grandmother had to pry this poor little girl off of Melvin, all the while lecturing her about the dangers of getting too close to strange dogs. And, certainly, the grandmother was right. The little girl was lucky she hugged Melvin instead of Chester. But most children, like most dogs, can see through the exterior shell and façade and directly into the soul. Melvin was a good soul, and she knew it. And the little girl was a good soul. And he knew it. So it was okay.

Throughout the day this little girl would "find" us again (surprise!) and smother Melvin with hugs, kisses and baby talk. Melvin just sat there and wagged his tail. During lunch time we were seated in a large grassy area. Sure enough, here came the little girl with her disapproving Grandmother in tow. She was carrying a chicken kabob with her. She ran to Melvin and threw her arms around him lovingly. Her chicken kabob was about an inch from Melvin's mouth. All he had to do was stick his tongue out just a tiny bit and he could've licked that chicken. It would have taken less effort to lick the chicken kabob than it would take to cough. Pretty much, no effort at all. He could've easily taken the whole kabob out of her hand. He could have swallowed it in one bite, stick and all. Many a hot dog had traveled from Melvin's mouth to his stomach without so much as a single tooth mark on it. He was almost like a professional sword swallower that actually swallows. But you know what he did? Nothing. He just sat there radiating love and patience and rocking that little girl's afternoon. His acts of self-restraint and love cemented his place in legend. To pass up a chicken kabob, a festival chicken kabob, after we'd been walking around for five hours? Best…Dog…in the WORLD!

But, again, we already knew this about him. We knew that, unlike Lassie, Melvin would never need to go and find help to rescue Timmy after he fell in the well. Melvin would fill in the well with rocks and dirt before Timmy could fall in it to begin with.

Melvin is much older now. He struggles with Old Dog Vestibular Disease, his eyesight and hearing are a thing of the past. There is no brown left on his face at all. It is totally white. And it looks like Father Time painted it on himself. Absolute perfection.

Melvin has some dementia issues and sometimes he gets lost in the living room, but he always finds his way. He's still Melvin. Still spreading love. Still making us smile. Still making the world a better place.

Sometimes I think about his old family and what they are missing. Sometimes I feel sorry for them and the fact that they didn't know the treasure that they had, how blind they were to the magic of Melvin. But then part of me feels like Melvin was meant to be here with us. Even if Melvin took up every minute of every day, I would always have time for him. A friend told me that when Melvin dies, "the angels will surely come down to escort him and then they'll be the lucky ones." I disagree. I mean, yes, the angels will be the lucky ones. But I think it will be Melvin who is doing the escorting, not the angels. Because it is polite and the right thing to do. And Melvin wouldn't have it any other way.

Don't Let The Door Hit 'Ya...

I know you are probably assuming that every dog we get, stays. In fact, this isn't true. Some of the dogs that have come here have not stayed. Here are a few of the more memorable ones.

Angel

I got a call from the shelter about a senior dog that really needed a home. I was told she was a little larger than we normally take, but because she was so old it wouldn't matter. Her activity level was so low we'd barely even know she was here. I was told she just needed a place to go live out the rest of her life, which probably wouldn't be that long. We are told that a lot, and it's almost never true.

Case in point; we have a little, eighteen-year-old Chihuahua named June. We got her in October and I was told she would probably live six weeks at the most because she was suffering from kidney failure, was extremely lethargic, could barely walk, had a constant wretched, awful sounding cough, and her body consisted of skin and bones. Like I said, we got her in October, and I named her June hoping she'd live long enough to see the month of June. Well, it is four "Junes" later and she is still here. She sleeps 98 percent of the time, but her cough is gone, she has put on a lot of weight so her body structure actually looks normal, and she has a routine of running in circles around my legs and jumping two feet into the air for her special, and extra, meal each night before I go to bed. For about five minutes a day, she has more energy than any dog in the house. So, when I'm told they probably won't live long, I don't always believe it.

When I was driving to get Angel, I wondered why are there so many shelter dogs named Angel? And why has every one of them I've met turned out to be so evil? But then I had new things to think about. When Angel came out with the volunteer I probably should have said something. Angel wasn't just a little larger than the dogs we normally take, she was much larger. Much. She looked to be some sort of lab mix. But that wasn't the reason I should have said something. I just didn't think she was old. When she first came out from the back room of the shelter, she jumped up and put her front paws on the front counter. And she wasn't just walking she was bouncing. But a lot of times what they are like at the shelter isn't a good representation of how they are in their day-to-day life. For all I knew, she could have been giving herself micro-fractures in her legs, jumping for joy, just so excited to get out of the shelter. She could have been one of those animals that, if they get their foot caught in a trap, would willingly chew off their foot just to escape. It happens.

Well, again, I try not to judge much of their behavior until after they get home and settle in, so I put her in the car. Actually, I didn't have to put her into the car, she jumped right into the back seat. Leapt. On her own. Now it has been my experience with senior dogs of all shapes and sizes that we typically have to hoist their back-ends into the car. Most seniors just can't lift their back legs more than a few inches off the ground. No matter how excited they might be, they just can't get their rears to cooperate. But not Angel. No. She was like a triple espresso-driven puppy on an agility course chasing a squirrel that is wearing bacon for a cape. She had energy to spare.

I got Angel home and she had no problems running up the front steps to our door. She took them two and three at a time. Again, typically we have to carry our dogs up those stairs or take them up around the side of the stairs and push them up the hill on to the side of the porch. Getting from the car to the door always takes at least a few minutes. Never a few seconds. Angel beat me to the door and sat there wagging her tail. She seemed really happy to be at a real home. I think she thought this was going to be awesome. But then I opened the front door.

Now, upstairs in the "no dog zone" there were probably four or five small dogs and Possum, our one "big old dog" that lives at the Sanctuary. Well, despite was I was told at the shelter, Angel didn't appear to like other dogs. Especially little dogs. The smaller the dog the more terrified she was. She immediately jumped on the couch to get away from tiny George, but when she did she just about landed on three pound Mildred who was napping on a small throw-pillow. When Angel saw Mildred she made a terrified leap onto the middle of the coffee table. This was not going well.

I decided to take her downstairs to see if that was any better. It wasn't. Angel got on the kitchen table and jumped from the kitchen table to the couch. When I was young, me and my siblings used to play a game called, "Hot Lava Monster." The whole point of the game was to jump around the room from chairs to sofas to pillows to cushions to tables to pretty much anything and not touch the floor. Because, of course, the floor was lava. If you touch the lava, the game is over. Well, it appeared this is exactly what Angel was doing. And she was doing it well. Obviously, she was a professional. I have never seen a "senior" dog be able to jump from the floor to the top of the kitchen table.

Running out of ideas, I thought she might enjoy meeting some dogs more her size, so I let in our Great Pyrenees/lab mix, Lillie Mae. Lillie was a little larger than Angel, but she is very sweet and most dogs love her. Angel didn't like her any more than she liked the little dogs and leapt from the couch onto the pass-through that goes to the kitchen and landed squarely on the kitchen counter. I just thought, "Now what?" She was so agile I couldn't dare let her out into our yard. We have a five foot fence that she could have cleared in her sleep. I decided to give her some "alone time" so she could calm down and try to adjust to her new surroundings, so I put her in our spare bedroom and closed the door.

She went insane. She was on top of the furniture in that room before I even closed the door. She got on the nightstand and broke the lamp. There wasn't even another dog in there but she was going crazy. So I opened the door and put a baby gate up so she could still see I was there and hoped that would help calm her down. Of course, she leapt over that baby gate in a single bound. It was only 7:00 in the evening, and we knew that we were going to be in for a long, long night. And it was indeed a long, long night.

The next morning, I did something I have never done before. I returned her to the shelter. Usually I'm willing to go through any amount of inconvenience and hassle to keep a dog. Erik, Oliver and I will alter our entire lives to make it work. But in this case, the only one more miserable than me was Angel. She hated it here. So away we went. They took her back into the kennel area and there was a lot of sighing and lamenting by the staff "that this was probably it for her. She would probably be euthanized. I mean, after all, she is an elderly dog." I already felt terrible returning her to the shelter and all of this made me feel even worse. I hardly slept at all that night. I kept thinking of things I should have tried. Maybe I could have sedated her until she got used to things, maybe I just hadn't given it enough time.

The next afternoon, after a lot of soul-searching and brain-storming and not being able to handle the label of "failure" that I'd placed upon myself, I called the shelter to tell them that I would be willing to give it another try. And guess what? As soon as the shelter had opened that day Angel had been adopted. Adopted by a

137

very active couple whose only other dog had just died. And these people loved to go hiking, camping and do agility courses.

Then the shelter told me that they had another dog they wanted me to take, instead. It was a male dog. They told me that he was a little larger than the dogs we normally take, but because he was so old it wouldn't matter. His activity level was so low we'd barely even know he was here. He just needed a place to go live out the rest of his life, which probably wouldn't be that long. I respectfully declined their generous offer and told them to have a nice day and I hung up the phone.

Yashik

So, I'm usually the person in our home who acquires the dogs. But when my husband told me about a guy he worked with who needed a home for a little, old dog who was I to say no? The dog was described as small (the person describing the dog held out their hands to about the size of a loaf of bread) and very old, maybe fifteen. The owner of the dog was moving to New York and didn't think the dog could make the big move. I'm always hesitant about these sorts of situations. I mean, not to sound callous or anything, but sometimes I think it is easier on the dog to be euthanized at that age, rather than be moved to a new environment away from the only human it has ever known. Sometimes I think people need to learn the lesson that there are worse things than death. This dog was also mostly blind, mostly deaf and had a few "small" tumors. If they were just fatty tumors, this wouldn't be a big deal. But being blind and deaf can sometimes make the transition even more difficult.

That being said, we've brought in many, many deaf and blind dogs from shelters that eventually adjust just fine, so I was willing to give this a shot. Well, we show up to pick up this little "size of a loaf of bread" dog. Turns out the dog was less the size of a loaf of bread and more the size of, well, a large dog. Not even a medium dog, but a large dog. It was also quite clear very early on that this dog had already been dead for some time. Sure, he was up and breathing. Sort of. But he should not have been alive in his condition. Medically and biologically, it shouldn't have been possible.

We were met on the porch by the owner of said dog (who also appeared to not be in very good physical condition) and apparently the guy was a hoarder, so we weren't privy to the inside of the apartment. However, we did catch a brief glimpse of the inside and it consisted of stacks of newspapers on either side of the door that reached up to the ceiling and allowed for a small entrance into what appeared to be a maze. It was worse than our garage. And that's saying a lot.

This dog's name was Yashik (named after a hockey player I'm told). I'm not sure what kind of dog Yashik was other than a dead zombie dog. He could barely walk. It took us five minutes to make the thirty foot stroll from the porch of the apartment to the car. Erik and I had to lift him into the backseat. Yashik promptly fell onto the floorboard and got wedged in between the seats. While trying to lift him back on the seat we felt what had to be about a twenty pound tumor on the side of this dog. That was mostly why he had no balance, the medicine ball tumor on his side was pulling him over. Yashik was very unhappy about being in the car and being away from his owner. And the fun was only beginning.

The rational thinking Hope (who doesn't make appearances too often, and certainly not where dog rescue is involved) would have said, "Hey, sorry, this dog is too big we can't take him." But I think Erik and I were both in such a state of shock that we just got the dog in the car and drove away in a strange trance. The only thing that brought us back to our senses was the smell of Yashik's breath. Okay. You must understand I'm no stranger to bad dog breath. In fact, I almost enjoy it. Most old dogs have bad teeth and bad dog breath. It is almost comforting to me. But this was levels and levels beyond normal bad dog breath. Ever heard of the kiss of death? Yashik's breath is the origin of that term. It smelled as though something inside of Yashik had died and he was breathing out the vile fumes. Without exaggeration, it smelled like Yashik was rotting from the inside out. But, as we were soon to find out, that wasn't the worst of his smells.

So we get the dog home after a horrifying ride of him repeatedly falling off the seat, getting stuck under the seat, getting wedged in between the seats and every other seat-related catastrophe that you could possibly imagine. Yes, we had brought a kennel for him to ride in, but even his tumor wouldn't have fit in our "small as a loaf of bread" dog kennel, let alone the entire dog. The whole trek was stressful, difficult, and depressing for everyone.

We made it home and pulled Yashik out of the car. He hated being in the car, but now that we were home he didn't want to get out. We eventually pulled him out and then we had the problem that he couldn't walk up stairs. In fact, he couldn't really walk at all. I'm guessing in his old home, his owner's hoarding issue kept him from walking around so he didn't have to do it much. And, when he did walk around, he didn't have to worry about falling over because the trash piled up on either side of him would keep him, generally, upright. He was very heavy so we decided to avoid the stairs and carried him up and around the side of the house to get in the front door.

Once inside he became even more depressed. It was apparent he hadn't ever been around other dogs and didn't want to be. And that, obviously, is sort of a problem at our house. He started pacing around (which looked like a very agitated drunk man being pulled over by a medicine ball sized tumor) and was falling into things within the first twelve seconds of being in the house. He knocked a table over and broke a lamp. Then he got stuck under the chair. Then he peed. Now, again, you should understand that I'm not new to dogs peeing in the house. It wasn't that he had peed in the house that freaked me out, it was the smell of his pee. Liquid death. That is the only way I can describe it. He was peeing out his rotten soul. Between his breath and his pee, the evil was trying to escape from both ends. And it smelled like it was succeeding. Mightily.

Well, we did our best to get him settled and then we went to bed. Erik and I didn't say a word to each other. We were still in that state of shock that we even had this dog. When I got up the next morning Yashik was not in the pen where I had left him. I couldn't find him anywhere. I had just started to panic when I heard something down in our mud room. He had fallen down the twelve stairs, climbed over stacks of boxes and was stuck back in the corner. I drug him back upstairs and then woke up Erik to have a talk. Now I'm not one to take euthanizing a dog lightly. I mean, I usually fall on the scale of "keep trying" rather than "let it go." But in this instance it wasn't about letting it go, it had already gone...long gone.

Erik had to call the owner and have a "talk" about Yashik. The conversation became very complicated very quickly. The owner got belligerent. He didn't think Yashik was in bad shape. He didn't seem to know what we were talking about. And the twenty pound tumor on his side? He had never noticed it. He was one of those pet owners who is in a bad state of denial, or can't bring themselves to go through the euthanasia. When Erik told the guy that Yashik really probably needed to be euthanized he suggested that we go do it for him. Now, this guy had been Yashik's owner for his entire life. I was angry. Yashik deserved to have the one person he loved there when he died, not a stranger. We offered to meet him at the vet and we even offered to pay for it, on the condition that he met us there so Yashik could be with him when he was put down. Or re-put down, as the case may be.

But the owner refused, so we ended up returning Yashik to his owner who did not take him to the vet. When he was confronted with the prospect of being there during the euthanasia, he said he didn't think it was time for Yashik to go. And that was true in the sense that it was way, way past time. I guess it was one of those situations where, technically, everyone was right.

Wolverine

Truman, our Great Pyrenees was just about six months old and we thought he might like to have a friend. With all of my preaching about how it's a bad idea to get a companion for another dog because it never works out, you think I would be able to follow my own advice, right? Well, I didn't. We had a bunch of little old dogs, but Truman was a young giant. Since there was such a difference in age and size I thought maybe another Great Pyrenees would make him really happy. I mean, he wasn't sad. Yet. But he could be. Soon. And the last thing we needed was a really big, really sad dog. So I felt the urge to be proactive and solve the problem before it was a problem.

I had forgotten how difficult puppies are to raise and Truman was a real handful, so we thought that an older dog would be the way to go. So I did what any crazy person would do...I turned to Craigslist. I immediately found an ad for an older male Great Pyrenees who needed a home. The ad indicated that the dog needed to be re-homed as soon as possible. I thought it would be great. It seemed like the perfect situation. He could mentor Truman and show him how to do his job as a Livestock Guardian. I pictured them becoming the best of friends. It was all turning into the Norman Rockwell painting of how I thought it should go. So Erik went and picked up Wolverine.

Erik drove all the way across town to meet Wolverine's owner at a dog park. When he pulled up, there was only one other car in the parking lot with a young woman standing next to it smoking a cigarette. Erik introduced himself and it turns out that, yes, it was Wolverine's owner. Sort of. Wolverine had belonged to her ex-boyfriend. Well, her ex-ex-ex-boyfriend. But now he was in prison and it looked like he wouldn't get out within the lifetime of the dog, and she had two dogs that belonged to her last boyfriend and now she had a new boyfriend and he had three dogs of his own and now they just have too many dogs.

She called for Wolverine and up from what must have been a fairly deep ditch emerged a beast. A horse. A beast of a horse in desperate need of a haircut. Erik was a little frightened.

When Erik and Wolverine got home, I was expecting this sweet older white puffy guy...which was not exactly what I got. The first thing I noticed about Wolverine was his heavily matted coat. He had mats on top of mats on top of mats. And it appeared that it was all held together by dirt. The second thing that I noticed was the look in Wolverine's eyes. The look was pure evil. Erik also had a look in his eyes. It was pure fear. And it was not lost on me the way that Wolverine's head was down under the plain of his shoulders. And his ears were down, too. And he was walking in this psycho-stalker sort of way. A controlled frenzy of pacing and slinking and darting that was not unlike a caged lion. And his tail was whipping back and forth. Not wagging. Just whipping in a slow, tortured, anxious sort of way. And, of course, he was huge. I instantly flashed back to the movie Cujo. Wolverine was not happy. Truman walked up to Wolverine, wagging his tail and acting like a happy puppy normally would. Wolverine growled and snapped at Truman. Truman yelped, freaked out, and ran full-speed out the back door. Wolverine hated our house, he hated Erik, he hated me, but worst of all he hated Truman.

We immediately separated Wolverine from all the little old dogs and away from Truman. Luckily our son wasn't home at the time. He was a toddler, Wolverine might have thought he was dinner. He continued to pace in a manic way. And growl. We didn't know what to do with him that night. He was still pacing and glaring. Erik decided to sleep upstairs so he could keep an eye on him. Literally. Erik slept the entire night with one eye open. Several times throughout the night, Erik would wake up and see Wolverine's nose about six inches away from his own. Erik told me later that his natural reaction was to scream out of fright, but he was worried that the sudden sound could cause Wolverine to eat his face. So he didn't. He just prayed that morning would come fast.

There was an uncomfortable phone call made the next morning and Wolverine went away. Back to the girl with the multitude of ex-boyfriends and ex-boyfriend's dogs. And hopefully, right now, Wolverine has been reunited with his original owner...where he belongs...safely tucked away in San Quentin State Prison.

That's Mister O.Possum To You

So, you may have guessed by our name, Little Old Dog Sanctuary, we take in little old dogs. Every now and then we end up with a medium sized dog. But Possum is not little. Possum is not medium. Possum is large. But he is old. He's very old. Ancient, even.

I initially was going to foster Possum for a few nights for a fellow rescuer who had just pulled him from the county shelter. When I made this offer I was thinking Possum was medium sized. I'm not sure why I thought this, but that is what I thought. So, I sent Erik to go and pick Possum up.

Erik called and told me that Possum was very large. And very unhappy. And very smelly. But none of these things really mattered because we were only going to have him for a few days. Well, Erik got Possum home but it wasn't easy getting him in. Possum has terrible arthritis. As in a "can barely walk" severe level of arthritis. And he was traumatized. He had been abandoned in an apartment after his owners were evicted. They got out, but left Possum behind. The landlord had to take Possum to the shelter. And he was in bad shape. He had a bad urinary tract infection, his teeth were rotten and he couldn't walk. And to add insult to injury he had just been taken to the vet that afternoon where he was poked, prodded and pricked. Possum doesn't like to be messed with in any way and he was fuming.

He came into the house and just sort of collapsed on the kitchen floor and stayed there for three days. I didn't know if he was just old, sick, dying, pissed off or all of the above. He didn't want the other dogs around him and just seemed horribly depressed.

Over the next few days, the only time Possum put any effort in to standing up was to go potty. Make no mistake…this dog was housebroken. Like, you could leave him unattended for two weeks and he'd hold it until his kidneys exploded. And after his kidneys exploded, he'd still hold it. Now, the reason I make such a big deal out of this is because being housebroken is such a rarity at our house. In fact, we sort of specialize in un-housebreaking dogs. If you want your dog un-housebroken, drop it off at our house and we'll have the job done in just a few hours. We have a lot of dogs that like to teach the new dogs bad habits. Just like in prison. But instead of learning how to rob banks, our new dogs learn how to go potty inside the house. But not Possum. Even though everyone else was peeing everywhere, and even though he can barely stand up to walk, he'd get up and drag himself outside. But then he would come back in, collapse on the floor like a dirty, matted old rug. He looked suicidal and a bit like road-kill. He was so stationary some of the other dogs took to peeing on him.

So I decided Possum might be happier if he went upstairs in the "no dog zone." The no dog zone is a room upstairs in which Erik ripped out the carpet and installed a hardwood floor during his only two days off in a five week span. And, at the time, he had a broken finger. Which he reminds Oliver and myself of every opportunity he gets. The no dog zone is sacred to Erik. Just ask him. And the concept wound up being a failure. You can ask him about that, too.

At this time, the only other dog in the "no dog zone" was a tiny Chihuahua named Mildred. Mildred had some issue with her legs so she could barely walk. She walked like Bambi after he was first born. Her legs twisted and she'd just fall over. She could somewhat navigate if she could lean up against a wall and walk. But none of this mattered to Mildred. She was totally fine with being carried around. She thought walking was way overrated. The strange thing was is that Mildred was found as a stray in the middle of a field in the middle of nowhere. Since she couldn't walk there is probably just one way she got there. And I'm guessing it wasn't running away from home for miles and miles on her own or being dropped off by a Falcon.

Anyway, during the day, Mildred lived on the couch in the "no dog zone." She couldn't get off the couch, so she wouldn't pee on the floor. This was the original reason to have a "no dog zone." So we would have a room with no dog pee. A room where you could walk in your socks or bare feet. Most people take this luxury for granted. If you are most people, you shouldn't take this for granted. You should count your blessings and be grateful.

But Possum was 100 percent housebroken. So why not keep him upstairs? We put Possum upstairs and then an amazing thing happened. He started making a miraculous transformation. His "flattened out" dirty rug imitation disappeared. He started becoming "dog-shaped" again. I had thought that he was in the process of dying, but I was wrong. Suddenly he looked normal. He didn't seem sick anymore. He was lifting his head off the ground. He was looking around like he might actually be considering living. And then he saw the tennis ball. It was like watching a toddler see the Disneyland Castle for the first time. Possum's eyes lit up and he looked about ten years younger. He could catch the ball in his mouth if you threw it well enough. And by "well enough" I mean right into his mouth. Sometimes he would even struggle to get up to run and catch it.

Possum had another reason to live. Erik. He loves Erik. Now, all the dogs love Erik, but they aren't "in love" with Erik. I'm typically the first choice of the dogs. They'll sit with Erik and sleep with Erik, but usually only if I'm not available. I always felt bad that Erik didn't have a dog that loved him best. Chester loves

Oliver more than anyone. And everyone else loves me. But Possum's life revolves around Erik. He is a very quiet dog. He sleeps the entire day except for his two potty breaks. He will occasionally bark at another dog if they get too close. But mostly he is silent and still. Until Erik comes home. Then he turns into a whiney, insistent attention hog. Possum sleeps right up against the front door all day waiting for Erik to open it. He wants to make sure he doesn't miss Erik, so he blocks the door all day. The minute Erik walks into the house Possum starts rubbing his eye juice on Erik's leg. Yes. You heard me correctly. Eye juice. Possum has it, and if he loves you, he expresses that love by rubbing it on you. He doesn't give kisses or anything like that, he just rubs his face on your leg. He could do this for hours with Erik. Erik comes in the door and has to just stand there with his hands full of groceries or papers, his sunglasses still on and stays there for twenty minutes while Possum rubs on him. He has no choice. That's just how it works.

Well, after seeing Possum's upstairs transformation I didn't have the heart to rehome him. He seemed fragile. I didn't think he could live through another heart-break. And I don't think anyone would have adopted him anyway. People aren't lining up to adopt an ancient crabby dog that can barely walk. Plus, how long could he really be expected to live?

Once it was decided that he was staying, we started experimenting with some meds for his arthritis. He's on the magic cocktail of pain meds. The big three...Gabapentin, Tramadol and Rimadyl. He takes about forty pills a day. Well, that may be an exaggeration. Maybe.

But between the tennis ball, the magic cocktail and his love for Erik I had to reevaluate my initial thought of how long he could really be expected to live. I'm thinking now he could live a long time. A really long time.

So here is the routine with Possum. He wakes up. He eats breakfast. He goes outside for five minutes and then barks to come back in. Then he goes to sleep up against the front door. He wakes up around three and goes potty and then it is back to sleep in front of the door. Then when Erik gets home he rubs his eye juice on him for twenty minutes. Then it begins. Possum starts whining. It is loud, it is annoying and it is never-ending.

Now usually if we have a dog that is barking nonstop or being really annoying, we'll spray them with a spray bottle we have filled with water. But Possum's arthritis is so bad I don't have the heart to spray him most of the time. It is painful to watch him try to get up in any kind of hurry. So mostly we just have to endure his arrangement of horrible howls, whines, barking and other annoying loud noises.

He also begs for our dinner. But not in a cute, sitting up on your butt, looking at you with big watery eyes kind of way. Nope. He just barks. And barks. And barks. Until you want to kill him. Until you want to kill yourself. Until blood pours from your ears. So you feed him. Which we realize is only rewarding his bad behavior. But you really can't take it. Oliver curses all of us on a nightly basis. "We should've never given him that chip!" He's convinced if we would have never given Possum that first potato chip, none of this would be an issue right now. He's probably right. But we've created a monster, and we have to live with him.

So we make elaborate meals for Possum. We make him a dog taco salad (a taco salad made for dogs, not a taco salad made from dogs). It consists of a tortilla bowl, dog food, lettuce, cheese, milk bones. Anything we can think of that will take time for him to eat. Anything that will fill his mouth so he can't bark. We get all of our food on the table and all get ready, forks and spoons in hand and then put Possum's food on the floor and we start eating as quickly as possible before Possum finishes his second dinner and starts barking again. Then we have to rush our plates back to the kitchen and erase any trace of food so he'll shut up. But Erik has to stay upstairs or else Possum will start whining for him.

The strange thing is, if Erik isn't here Possum is silent. Oliver and I can eat dinner and Possum never makes a peep. If Erik works all night, I forget we even have Possum. It is something about Erik that makes Possum cry and misbehave. Like a child who wants attention, good or bad, Possum acts up only when Erik is home. He doesn't care enough about me and Oliver to put on the big show for us. Of course Erik believes none of this, but it is true.

As much as I think he could live a long time, Possum has had many close calls with death. There have been several occasions when Erik and I start preparing ourselves for the inevitability of Possum's demise. First we thought it would be because he just wouldn't be able to get up anymore. Possum isn't a great candidate for wheels because his front legs don't work much better than his back legs. There was a period of time where he could just barely get up and we thought maybe the time was coming but we added in some additional mid-day meds and pretty soon he was back to his normal self (don't get me wrong, his "normal self" isn't anything astonishing, but it doesn't warrant being euthanized, either). We can tell if he is doing well with his arthritis if he can go up and down the stairs on the front porch without falling. Possum is so worried about being abandoned that you can let him out the front door, he'll go potty on the porch or in the front yard, and then he's back at the front door crying to be let in. He rarely stays out more than five minutes. And if Possum barks, our Great Pyrenees, Lillie Mae starts howling. Between the two of them, it is pretty apparent within a one-mile radius of the house when Possum wants back inside.

So now that we had the arthritis under control and that wasn't going to kill him, he got these really nasty things called hygromas on his elbows. These are just big lumps that burst and are gross and messy. It looks like a crime scene when one of these things opens up. Blood everywhere. When the flow is reduced to a minor leak, you are left with just a big, open sore. Like a crater on the moon. I've never experienced these before. I guess they are common in large dogs, but remember, we are Little Old Dog Sanctuary…Chihuahuas just don't get these sorts of things. These nasty sores can also result from lying on hard surfaces. Now understand that pretty much our entire house is covered in dog beds, blankets, pillows and other assorted soft stuff. Clean, comfy, cushiony soft stuff. I usually do six loads of laundry a day for the dogs. So the dogs always have choices. Lots and lots of choices. But Possum won't have any of it. He insists on laying on the hard tile floor next to the front door. I tried putting a blanket there for him to lay on and he went to the other side of the room and just glared at me. We got him a huge orthopedic bed for his arthritis. He wouldn't get near it so we had to put him on top of it. Possum doesn't like to be touched, not even by the love of his life, Erik. So putting him on the bed was traumatic. He immediately got off the bed. I couldn't even shove a towel under his elbow. If anything soft or comfortable touches him, he freaks out. If a blanket is even near him he retreats as far away as possible. I had never really encountered this before. The little dogs I'm used to are like the Princess in The Princess and the Pea story. If they aren't on or under one hundred and twenty six blankets, they might get a bruise. Or a chill. Or both.

In an effort to get the arm craters to heal on Possum, first we tried a bandage. In order to get the bandage on his elbow (which was leaving a blood and pus trail throughout Erik's coveted no dog zone) we had to muzzle him. We don't usually resort to such methods, but you know, sometimes it takes tough love. Well, that, and Erik is tired of getting bitten. But even with the muzzle, the bandaging did not go well. And he ripped the bandage off the minute we had the muzzle off of his face. Then he wouldn't eat for two days. We couldn't tell if it was from the hygroma or the muzzle. I had him on a whopping dose of antibiotics and got this antiseptic spray that I would use on his elbow if he was sleeping. That was all we could do for it. Then I found this device online made for this exact problem. It consisted of these two padded "sleeves" and a harness type device that went over his back so he couldn't get the sleeves off. Thankfully the company donated it to us. We got it in the mail, muzzled Possum and put it on him. He was mad. I mean, really mad. He wouldn't lie down. He paced for two hours straight (remember that Possum rarely even gets up, so pacing around the room was a very bad sign). He cried non-stop for those two hours. It was awful.

151

I suck at tough love. I'm just not wired for it. I was doing really well to keep those things on Possum's elbows for two hours. I knew it was for his own good. I knew I had to be strong. But I couldn't do it. I guess if the elbow sores were going to kill him that would be better than the elbow pads killing him. I took them off, he growled at me, and then went to sleep for eighteen hours straight. We thought we were going to lose him this time for sure. But, he rallied. Again. In the end, his elbows healed with little to no assistance from us.

That incident taught us a lesson. That lesson was, just leave well enough alone. That I shouldn't always try to fix things. There are many things I would like to do for Possum. But trying to do all of these things could send him over the edge and he is too old to go over the edge. He may not come back. It is a delicate balance sometimes and we need to respect and honor that.

However, there is one element in Possum's life that requires us to take action every few months, and we all hate it. I hate it, Erik hates it, and Possum certainly hates it. We have to trim Possum's toenails. Shridhar Chillal (a human being, born in 1938 in India) holds the world record for the longest fingernails. They measure a total of 20 feet and 2 ¼ inches. Possum's nails come in a very close second to Shridhar's accomplishment. A main difference between the two, however, is that Possum hates to have his nails touched. Or his feet. Or his legs. Or his hips, for that matter. So Erik has to muzzle him and Possum's eyes get as large as saucers and he freezes up and I'm pretty sure that he stops breathing. Erik trims the nails down as fast as he can and removes the muzzle as fast as he can and, no matter what, it never seems like he is able to do it fast enough. Possum always looks and acts like he has been emotionally fractured. It is beyond sad.

As I'm writing this, Possum is lying in front of the door on the hard tile floor. His fur is dirty, he could use a brushing and a bath. His toenails are too long. What I wouldn't give to be able to brush his teeth. But he is alive, he is dreaming of the moment when

Erik comes home, and he is happy. And in the end, ultimately, that is what really matters the most.

The Fountain of Youth

I remember that I got George on Halloween. He was my "treat" for the day. I drove to the shelter not knowing what to expect. I remember walking to the kennel and seeing this tiny little guy. He pranced up to the gate wagging his tail. He was about five pounds with gorgeous blonde Farrah Fawcett hair. Big and bold and beautiful. But mostly big. If "he" were a "she" I would have definitely considered naming her Farrah. But he wasn't. So Gorgeous George seemed perfectly appropriate. My husband told me that Gorgeous George was a famous wrestler from decades ago. But I kept the name, anyway. My Gorgeous George was a long haired Chihuahua. He was old, probably fifteen and had come in as a stray. I plucked him up, he seemed relieved. Then we went home. As near as I could tell, George didn't know any wrestling moves, neither real nor fake.

George had no teeth and his tongue hung out the side of his mouth in an adorable way. George was old but he was still very active and friendly. He loved to bark in this old man sort of raspy way. And then it became more of a cough than a rasp. And that was funny because I hadn't noticed the cough at the shelter or on the drive home. It was almost as if he was keeping it a secret until we got home, just in case the indication that he might be ill would make me change my mind. Little did he know that something like that usually has the opposite effect.

Well, "no big deal" I thought. Kennel cough. Almost every dog we get has some form of kennel cough from being in the shelter. Old dogs are especially prone to it. And old dogs who have been mistreated or malnourished or are stressed out, well, it is almost like there is something wrong with the dog if they don't have it. But, other than that little cough, George was a lively little guy. He liked attention, but not in a needy way. He was a very independent, "in charge" kind of guy. I loved him immediately. I got George the day before we had to put down our beloved five year old Great Pyrenees, Truman, who was suffering from bone cancer. We had been trying to keep Truman going for about an extra six months, but when it's time, it's time. He was our giant, reliable, loving, trusted guard dog. George saved me from drowning in my grief over Truman.

A few months went by and George's cough remained. I know kennel cough can be stubborn and sometimes takes several months to fully go away. But then the snow melted, the leaves came out on our lilac bush, our front porch was taken over by baby chipmunks playing tag, the flowers started to bloom; yet one single, solitary thing remained the same…George's cough. It was dry and raspy, and should have gone away by now.

So, off to the vet we went. George's lungs sounded fine. Clear. No fluid. He had a bad heart murmur, but that's not much of a surprise. If our vet had told me he didn't have a heart murmur, now that would've been a surprise! Just like kennel cough, heart murmurs are pretty much a prerequisite for living here. Our vet wanted to do some x-rays. I remember her coming back in the room and showing them to me. I was informed that George had the worst collapsing trachea that she had ever seen. Now, I get that comment a lot from my vet about our dogs. "This dog you brought in here today has the worst case of (fill in your choice of death-causing malady) that I've ever seen." Then she showed me the tiny needle thin tube that George was breathing through. I was shocked. I couldn't believe that he was even able to breathe at all.

She said he probably wouldn't live long (this is also a standard phrase we hear when visiting the vet). She prescribed him some cough medicine and some steroids to see if that would help. There was a very expensive complicated surgery that can be done on a collapsing trachea. It is only done by a few doctors in the country and the results are mixed. The success rate for a young and otherwise healthy dog is fairly low. Well George was fifteen and had a terrible heart, so no surgery for him. We know all about bad hearts in older dogs and how it limits our options when it comes to things like surgery and other treatments. So the vet gives us another treatment, one that we are quite familiar with. "The best thing you can do for George is to keep him as calm as possible and make him comfortable and happy." And then we all laughed. He is a Chihuahua, hardly the breed standard for calm in the dog world. Well, George was already very happy, so we didn't have to worry about that. And he was comfortable as far as having several comfy places to sleep with cozy blankets and pillows and plenty of food and water. He coughed almost nonstop, but it didn't seem to bother him much. And if it's not bothering him, then it's not bothering us. His cough became much like a ticking clock does for other people, you just don't hear it anymore.

He spent his days barking and coughing and then barking some more. He refused to take his cough medicine. We had to have his medicine made in a compound form (because of his tiny size) at one of the few compounding pharmacies remaining in Colorado. The medicine wound up being sort of expensive, but they made it beef flavored to help entice him to take it. And, of course, he wouldn't touch it. As a matter of fact he hated it. I put it down his throat a few times against his will, but that stressed him out so much that it would throw him into a coughing fit which would be much worse than if he didn't have the medicine to begin with, so what was the point? We finally gave up on the expensive beef flavored cough suppressant. He would take his steroids in a hot dog, so at least we were doing something.

Sometimes we have to decide if the cure is worse than the illness and measure the stress and anxiety of the proposed cure. In regards to an old dog, especially with a heart murmur or brain tumor or organ failure, our job is not to cure, but to just provide hospice care, love and happiness. It isn't always in the best interest in the dog to pursue surgeries, radical treatments and long-shot remedies. We always choose quality over quantity. With George we knew his days were numbered and we didn't want him to spend those hiding under the couch from us lest he have beef flavored syrup forced down his throat. I can understand doing this to a young dog, but George had already had a long life. And I wasn't going to torture him because I wanted him to live even longer.

Dogs live in the moment, and having all of your final moments be filled with fear or anxiety is no way to live. If that is all they have, then it would probably be in their best interest to have them put to sleep. Or, at the very least, I know that if I was very sick with a terminal illness and that the rest of my life was to be spent living in fear and anxiety, then I would absolutely want to be put to sleep. Besides, fear and anxiety can turn their pain in to a whole new level of suffering that they'd never had experienced before. We can keep most of their pain in check using a combination of the "Big Three" (Tramadol, Gabapentin, Rimidyl). But there is a limit to what even these magical pharmaceuticals can provide.

So the days and months went by. George was doing well. He was still coughing, but it hadn't gotten worse and he was happy. Well, I guess I thought he was happy, but I hadn't yet seen the full extent of George's happiness. He had already lived longer than he was supposed to, and we were waiting for the inevitable "crash" that the terminal dogs always experience. And we were still going to have to wait.

In my typical fashion of making poorly thought out choices, or, as my husband calls it, "impulsive choicing," when I got an opportunity to foster a small pregnant dog from the county shelter (about to have babies any day now) I jumped on it. I know the world doesn't need another puppy, but I couldn't stand the thought of this little mama having all her babies euthanized so close to her due date. She came from the same shelter that George (and many other of our dogs) came from. So I drove to pick her up. They had her in a garage part of the shelter to keep her as isolated as possible from kennel cough, parvo and distemper since she couldn't be vaccinated. I named her Priscilla.

Priscilla was a very young terrier. Her fur was beige and white and stringy. Except for her giant, brown eyes, she was skin, bones and babies. I carried her out to the car and she radiated gratefulness. I brought her home and put her on a warm couch. She stretched out and took a two hour nap. So much for having to try to get her used to living at the Sanctuary. She was beyond comfortable. She was safe. And she knew it.

Now, at the time, George was sort of the sentry of our home. He slept on his ladybug pillow pet by the front door. He liked other dogs and welcomed each new dog we would take in but he had a special interest in Priscilla. It was almost as if he were the father of those babies. He was very protective of Priscilla while she was pregnant and kept a close eye on everything she did. Priscilla being in the house seemed to calm George down a bit. It was like he had a job, and part of the job description was to simply remain calm.

We, on the other hand, were a little more nervous. We are in the land of old dogs, and are stocked for such. We are not stocked to deal with dogs giving birth. We are stocked for pain relief, upset tummies and terminal illness. We are stocked for dying and death, not birth and brand new life. So we got a whole box together of the traditional whelping supplies: paper towel, iodine, scissors, gauze, plastic bulb, eye dropper, puppy feeding formula, bottles...the works. Stuff we need now (and thought) we would never need again, though it sure came in handy with those orphaned mice. We made Priscilla a whelping box, the perfect whelping box. Priscilla was not the least bit interested in it but George promptly climbed in and sat vigil. At the time, we thought he was being a perfect gentleman and keeping it warm for her and her puppies. But in retrospect, I guess he knew she wasn't going to have her babies in that box, so he might as well get some use out of it. George was always a practical dog.

So, we all waited and watched Priscilla for any signs that she would have the babies. We had set up a futon on the floor of the living room so my husband could sleep up there and keep an eye on Priscilla. There were too many dogs in the bedroom, so we had to put her in the "No Dog Zone." So now we were up to four dogs in the "No Dog Zone," which we should have probably renamed the "Limited Dog Zone." But Priscilla was comfortable, and that is what mattered the most. George would sleep as close to Priscilla as he could. It seemed that George knew we were expecting something. Something more than my husband's attempt to keep the dogs out of at least one room in the house ending in abject and utter failure.

Well, the hours and then the days went by. Still no babies. And she wasn't showing any signs of having them. Loss of appetite, anxiety, nesting. Nothing. We could feel the babies kicking, so we knew that they were alive. And as long as they were alive, we knew that she would have them when she was supposed to have them, and not a minute sooner. That is how it works.

Then one night I was sleeping when my husband ran into the room to wake me up…Pricilla had already had three puppies! I guess Erik had come home from work at about midnight and Priscilla greeted him at the door as usual. He did his usual evening chores and then went and took a shower and when he came back upstairs to get into bed, about an hour and a half after he had gotten home, he threw back the covers on the futon and there was Priscilla, having babies under the blankets right in the middle of the futon. George had been correct about her not having the babies in the whelping box. And Erik had to return to work in a few hours, so I supervised the rest of the delivery process. Priscilla had two more babies that night, five total.

We officially ditched the nesting box as a place for the puppies, though we kept it up for the next few weeks for George to sleep in. The futon was the new official puppy bed. Strategically placed pillows and towels and comforters kept everyone safe and secure. And the "no dog zone" was officially "no more."

As a new mother, Priscilla didn't want any of the other dogs near her babies. But George was determined. He would crawl on his belly from the nesting box on the other side of the room and inch closer and closer to the puppies on the futon over a span of several hours. About the time that George would round the sofa and get within six or seven feet of the futon, Priscilla would notice him and chase him off, back to the nesting box. Then George would start the "crawl" all over again. I think he might have eventually been successful, but his cough kept giving away his location.

Sometimes he got close enough to see the babies in the middle of the futon. I would watch him watching them. I wasn't sure at first if he just loved looking at them or was planning on eating them. Maybe he didn't either.

George's covert operation went on for several weeks. But by this time Priscilla's interest in her puppies was waning. The puppy's teeth had grown in and their toenails had developed in to bona-fide, razor-sharp implements of destruction. So nursing them had become difficult and painful and, really, not necessary any more since we had started them on puppy food mush. And they were starting to crawl around. And then they were stumbling around. And then they were walking around. So, if Priscilla was out of the room taking a break, George would run to the puppies, pin them down and lick them. I think he felt like he was the father-figure in their life and he needed to do what he could to take care of them, which included plenty of love.

When the puppies started running around and playing, George had to take his puppy-rearing to the next level and he became the disciplinarian. He would snap at them and tackle them to make them behave. We knew that George was not getting any better and we didn't want to stress him out so we always gave him an option to escape to a quieter room and he could've gotten away from them at any time, but chose not to. He spent all of his time right in the middle of their playing, fighting and sleeping. He was teaching them manners. He was teaching them proper socialization. He was teaching them love. He was teaching them the way of the world. The way of George's world. George was on a mission. And he was happy.

George's life revolved around the puppies. George went from being on the verge of death to living with a definite purpose. He was so happy. His cough was getting worse, but he was too busy to be sick. He was too busy to die. It was like he had gotten his dream job. The color of George's parachute was puppy. And the puppies loved him even though he snapped at them and pinned them down every chance he got. He didn't allow too much rough-housing. He was like their old Grandpa with the smoker's cough and the sage wisdom that he had to pass on to future generations.

George died from heart failure when the puppies were exactly seven weeks old. I have to say I'm glad he went before the puppies were rehomed a week later. If George had actually planned his time of death, he couldn't have done it any more perfectly. Somehow, it was better that he died of heart failure than a broken heart.

We now have a new litter of puppies and I wish I had George here as a nanny. And Erik wishes he had a "no dog zone." Neither of us will ever get our wish. And you know what? That's okay.

Happily Ever After

I would love to be able to tell you I have the best job in the world. I would also like to be able to tell you that where I am now started out as a deliberate, well thought out plan. I would like to tell you those things, I really would. Truth be told, I'm not exactly sure how I ended up here.

Besides filling the needs of the dogs, I respond to the dozens of emails I get every day. I can pretty much divide the emails into two categories. Category One – Take this dog off my hands or else I will have to have it killed. Category Two – You are amazing and you have my dream job. The volume of Category One emails strongly outweighs the Category Two emails.

For the Category One email people, all I can really say is that the Sanctuary is full. Overly full. Beyond overly full. And we don't take owner surrenders, for the simple reason that I can't say no. So, I figured if I had a "rule" then I wouldn't have to fret over it. But, of course, I still do. Because most of these emails contain these two sentences. The beginning sentence is, "It isn't fair to the dog for us to keep it" (as if it is fair to the dog to give it away) and end with this threat, "If you can't take our dog we'll be forced to euthanize." This keeps me awake at night. I know I can't take them all, but I agonize over not being able to. For the Category Two people...thank you for the compliment. But, to put you in my reality for a moment, imagine seeing this job posting:

Wanted: Executive Director; Assistant Executive Director; Intern; fundraiser; accountant; webmaster; administrative assistant; caretaker; vet tech; housekeeper, etc. needed to run a hospice/sanctuary for senior and special needs dogs and abandoned farm animals. Must love old, messed up dogs that won't necessarily love you back. Must be experienced in dealing with all types of fluids and solids - urine, vomit, blood, saliva, pig snot, chicken poop, diarrhea etc. Must be able to deal effectively with your own anxiety, worry and heartbreak on a regular basis without it having a negative influence on your friends and family. Funding is extremely limited, so you will have to run the Sanctuary out of your home. You will not get a week, day, hour or minute off. Don't bother planning a vacation because you will never get one. From the moment you wake up (or are awoken) until the moment you fall asleep (or pass out from exhaustion), you will spend all of your time cleaning floors, as "incontinent" and "not housebroken" are adjectives commonly associated with our residents, administering thousands of medications, changing water, cleaning beds and bedding (five laundry load minimum per day,) breaking up fights and "misunderstandings," checking each dog for unusual things like lumps, bumps and wounds, giving life-saving fluids and injections, shaving messy butts and any other glamourous dog related function you could possibly imagine. A car is required, but you are only allowed to go to the vet or get dog food and immediately return to the Sanctuary that will have been totally trashed, even if you were only gone for twenty five minutes. Other duties include respectfully answering dozens of emails each day from people wanting to dump their dogs at your Sanctuary, and standing your ground, firmly, when people offer to drive their dog to the Sanctuary from all the way across the country. And, oh, by the way, they are willing to start driving immediately. So you must be willing to have your property plastered with "No Trespassing" signs so that if you catch someone dumping a dog, they can be charged with multiple crimes (and you get the extra bonus of being able to legally attack them with a pitchfork). It is also imperative that you figure out a way to fund the Sanctuary, keep up with the accounting, design a website, maintain the website, post on social media in an attempt to remain relevant and send out thank you letters to the people who are actually kind enough to help you out. Other mandatory qualifications include multi-tasking between the animals, your young son and your husband. Your body must require only minutes of sleep per day, and when you do sleep, you must do so with one eye open. You must be able to calmly deal with stressful situations. And, finally, you must have excellent customer service skills, even when you are at your wits end. The salary is absolutely, positively nothing with matching benefits. In fact, you'll end up paying every penny you have to make the Sanctuary function. The hours are 24/7 with no sick days or holidays. You must make a commitment for the lifetime of all these animals. Looking to fill this position immediately, if not sooner.

Would you jump to apply to this job? I don't blame you if your answer is no. But somehow, for me, it feels like the perfect job in the world. Except the salary. That could use some work.

I have always loved old things. I never understood why anyone would want something new when they could have something old. I rarely buy anything new. The only things I have that aren't old would be my husband (who is one year younger than I am) and my son. I still have one of my first stuffed animals. It was a Christmas gift from Santa when I was four years old. His name is Ed the Elephant. He is worn down and I've had to replace his entire body several times. But he smells like he always has (home), and I am deeply in love with him. He is permanently formed into a hug. I've slept with him every night since I was little, so he is in the shape of my arms being wrapped around him for so many years. I wouldn't trade him for all the money or all the new stuffed elephants in the world.

I feel this same way about old dogs. There is something about an old dog that just makes me melt. Is it the cloudy, trusting eyes? The frosted face? The smell of dirty teeth? Maybe all of these things. But I know it is certainly their spirit. I can't stand to see these old dogs end up in shelters. There are so many reasons people dump their dogs at shelters. They are moving, they had a baby, the dog had an accident in the house. It seems in our society, we have no loyalty or feel no responsibility to the elderly. When they become inconvenient, we "get rid of them" and get something new. Like a puppy. It is a vicious cycle that gets repeated over and over again.

I haven't always been good with death. When my first dog died, Franny, I didn't think I was going to be able to work through that much grief ever again. But I had twelve other dogs at the time, so I knew I was going to have to. And I did, and I do. I wouldn't say you get used to it, but you certainly get better at it. And really, what's to be afraid of? Death is inevitable. It is going to happen to all of us. So it is how we honor and cherish this passing that matters. I feel honored to help these animals on to their next journey. I feel grateful that I have had the ability and opportunity to fill the last bit of their lives, whether it is days or years, with love and dignity. Each dog, no matter what their lives have been like up to this point, will leave this world knowing love and adoration, knowing that they mattered. I feel blessed that the universe trusted me with all of these little souls. And whenever it gets too painful or too hard, I just think how much harder it would have been if these dogs had died alone and unloved in a shelter. To not do what I do is insurmountably harder than to do what I do. I give them an opportunity to live. I give them hope. And my name is Hope. When I feel like I can do this no more, I take a deep breath and say, "My name is Hope." I am reminded of who I am, what I am, and my purpose. And most importantly, how in my own small way, I can make things better.

I want to feel like my life has made a difference. I want to feel like I've done something that mattered. I picture my death bed often, but not in some kind of twisted, morbid way. No. It is a good way for me to check in with myself to make sure I am on the right course. The right path. What I don't want is to be on my death bed and only be able to say, "My house was always clean, always immaculate. Everything always smelled good and I kept up with the Jones' even better than Mr. and Mrs. Jones did."

I want to say, "I helped make the world a better place in my own small way. I honestly did what I could, and then some, even when it wasn't fun. I made a difference. A positive difference. And, if anything, my house was bursting with love, life, and hope."

And it is. It really is. And I am grateful for it. All of it. The good, the bad, and the ugly. And if there is a Rainbow Bridge, when I die, I fully expect to be trampled and licked by dozens and dozens of happy dogs. I want to be able to look all of those dogs directly in the eye and say "And we all lived happily ever after."

Because we did.

71536864R00105

Made in the USA
Lexington, KY
21 November 2017